Hindu Marriage Act of 1955

CHAPTER I
PRELIMINARY

1. Short title and extent.-(1) This Act may be called THE HINDU MARRIAGE ACT, 1955.

(2) It extends to the whole of India except the State of Jammu and Kashmir, and applies also to Hindus domiciled in the territories to which this Act extends, who are outside the said territories.

Objects and Reasons:- The words "domiciled in India" have been changed to "domiciled in the territories to which this act extends" to make the position clear, so that the law will be applicable to all Hindus with such domicile, who may, for the time being, be outside the said territories-whether they be in Jammu and Kashmir or outside India altogether.

2. Application of Act.- (1) This Act applies-

(a) to any person who is a Hindu by religion in any of its forms or developments, including a Virashaiva, a Lingayat or a follower of the Brahmo, Prarthana or Arya Samaj;

(b) to any person who is a Buddhist, Jaina or sikh by religion; and

(c) to any other person domiciled in the territories to which this Act extends who is not a Muslim, Christian, Parsi or Jew by religion, unless it is

----

1. The Act has been extended to (1) Dadra and Nagar Haveli by regulation 6 of 1963 (w.e.f.1-7-1965) and (2) Pondicherry by regulation 7 of 1963 (w.e.f.1-10-1963); Sikkim by Noti.No.S.O.311(E), dated 28-4-1989 (w.e.f.1-5-1989).

This Act has also been applied to the State of Jammu & Kashmir by the J & K. Hindu Marriage Act, 1955 (J & K. Act 8 of 1955) subject to certain modifications. Now the 1955 Act has been repealed by J & K. Act 4 of 1980. Hence, this Act does not apply to J & K.

Proved that any such person would not have been governed by the Hindu Law or by any custom or usage as part of that law in respect of any of the matters dealt with herein if this Act had not been passed.

Explanation.- The following persons are Hindua, Buddhists, Jainas or Sikhs by religion, as the case may be:-

(a) any child, legitimate or illegitimate, both of whose parents are Hindus, Buddhists, Jainas of Sikh by religion;

(b) any child, legitimate or illegitimate, one of whose parents is a Hindu, Buddhist, Jaina of Sikh by religion and who is brought up as a member of the tribe, community, group or family to which such parent belongs or belonged; and

(c) any person who is a convert or re-convert to the Hindu, Buddhist, Jaina or Sikh religion.

(2) Notwithstanding anything contained in sub-section (1), nothing contained in this Act shall apply to the members of any Scheduled Tribe within the meaning of clause (25) of article 366 of the Constitution unless the Central Government, by notification in the Official Gazzette, otherwise directs.

(3) The expression "Hindu" in any portion of this Act shall be construed as if it included a person who, though not a Hindu by religion, is, nevertheless, a person to whom this Act applies by virtue of the provisions contained in this section.

State Amendment-[Pondicherry].- In its application to the Union territory of Pondicherry, in S.2, after sub-S.(2), insert the following sub-section, namely.-

"(2-A) Notwithstanding anything contained in sub-section (1), nothing contained in this act shall apply to the Renoncants of the Union territory of Pondicherry."- See Regn. 7 of 1963, S.2(w.e.f.1-10-1963).

Update on 19th March,2010
COMMENTS

Where both the parties to the petition were two Tribals, who otherwise profess Hinduism, held, their marriage being out of the purview of Hi ndu Marriage Act, 1955 in light of section 2(2) of the Act were governed only by their Santal Customs and usage: Surajmani Stell Kujur V. Durge Charan Hansdah A.I.R. 2001 S.C.938.

In view of S.19 read Alongwith Ss. 1 and 2, the Hindu Marriage Act, 1955 applies to all Hindus who got married according to Hindu rites, irrespective of domicile and / or residence: Nitaben v. Dhirendra Chandrakanth Sukhla (1984) 1 D.M.C. 252; (1984-1) 25 Guj. L.R. 276.

   3. **Definitions.-** In this Act, unless the context otherwise requires,-

   (a) the expression "custom" and "usage" signify any rule which, having been continuously and uniformly observed for a long time, has obtained the force of law among Hindus in any local area, tribe, community, group or family:
   Provided that the rule is certain and not unreasonable or opposed to public policy; and
   Provided further that in the case of a rule applicable only to a family it has not been discontinued by the family;

   (b) "district court" means in any area for which there is a City Civil Court, that Court, and in any other area the principal Civil Court of original jurisdiction, and includes any other Civil court which may be specified by the State Government, by notification in the Official Gazette, as having jurisdiction in respect of the matters dealt with in this Act;

   Objects and Reasons.- The definition of "district court" has been modified to make it clear that where there is a City Civil Court, it is that Court alone which shall have jurisdiction under this law. By another amendment, the power to notify inferior Courts as districts courts for the purposes of this law is a sought to be vested in the State Government instead of in the Central Government, as originally proposed.

   (c) "full blood" and :half blood" – two persons are said to be related to each other by full blood when they are sescended from a common ancestor by the same wife and by half blood when they are sescended from a common ancestor but by different wives;

(d) "uterine blood" – two persons are said to be related to each other by uterine blood when they are descended from a common ancestress but by different husbands;

Explanation.- In clauses (c) and (d), "ancestor" includes the father and "ancestress" the mother;

(e) "prescribed" means prescribed by rules made under this Act,

(f) (1) "sapinda relationship" with reference t any person extends as far as the third generation (inclusive) in the line of ascent through the mother, and the fifth (inclusive) in the line of ascent through the father, the line being traced upwards in each case from the person concerned, who is to be counted as the first generation;

(ii) two persons are said to be "*sapindas*" of each other if one is a lineal ascendant of the other within the limits of *sapinda* relationship, or if they have a common lineal ascendant who is within the limits of *sapinda* relationship with reference to each of them;

(g) "degrees of prohibited relationship" – two persons are said to be within the "degrees of prohibited relationship"-

(i) if one is a lineal ascendant of the other; or

(ii) if one was the wife or husband of a lineal ascendant or descendant of the other; or

(iii) if one was the wife of the brother or of the father's or mother's brother or of the grandfather's or grandmother's brother of the other; or

(iv) if the two are brother and sister, uncle and niece, aunt and nephew, or children of brother and sister or of two brothers or of two sisters;

Explanation:- For the purposes of clause (f) and (g), relationship includes-

(i) relationship by half or uterine blood as well as by full blood;
(ii) illegitimate blood relationship as well as legitimate;
(iii) relationship be adoption as well as by blood;
and all terms of relationship in those clauses shall be construed accordingly.

Objects and reasons.- The definition of "prohibited degrees" and "sapinda relationship" are on the lines of the Rau committee's Report. As has been pointed out by that committee, the strict rule prohibiting marriages within the limits of sapinda relationships defined in the Smritis (seven and five degrees) have been considerably relaxed by custom and the limits have, therefore, been reduced to five and three degrees, as is generally recognized now. A definition of "prohibited degrees" is also necessary because there is the greatest diversity among Hindus in different parts of India as to what are the prohibited degrees for marriage. The usual rule is that the parties should not be sapindas of each other. Not only, however, has the sapinda relationship been interpreted in different ways by different authors, but the rule itself has been subjected to modification by custom. Some kind of limit has, therefore, to be provided to prevent incestuous marriages, subject to judicially recognized customs or well-established customs which satisfy the requirements of the definition of that expression.

Joint Committee Report:- The definition of prohibited degrees in sub-clause (g) has been expanded so as to include the brother's widow, the paternal or maternal uncle's widow, the widow of the grand-father's or grand-mother's brother and the children of brother and sister. In the opinion of the Joint Committee, marriage within such relationships should be discouraged; but wherever there is a custom to the contrary, ample recognition of such custom is contained in clause.

COMMENTS

The customs/usage is to be tested on the touchstone of the definition of custom/usage. As per reading of the definition it is to be found that there are five ingredients of the aforesaid definition, namely (i) it has been continuously and uniformly observed for a long time; (ii) it has obtained the force of law among Hindus in any local area, tribe, community, group or family; (iii) it is certain; (iv) it is not unreasonable or opposed to public policy; and (v) in case of a rule applicable only to a family, it has not been discontinued by the family: Sharad Dutt v. Kiran (1997) 2 D.M.C. 643: (1997) 69 del.L.T. 510.

4. Overriding effect of Act:- Save as otherwise expressly provided in this Act,-

(a) any text, rule or interpretation of Hindu Law or any custom or usage as part of that law in force immediately before the commencement of this Act shall cease to have effect with respect to any matter for which provisions is made in this Act;

(b) any other law in force immediately before the commencement of this Act shall cease to have effect in so far as it is inconsistent with any of the provisions contained in this Act.

COMMENTS

In view of sub-S. (2) of S. 29, overriding effect of S.4(a) will not operate subject to, of course, the existence of custom. Thus, where customary divorce is proved to be in existence in any caste, the custom is saved. G.Thimma Reddy v. Special Tahsildar Land Reforms, Adoni II (1993) 1 An W.R.2: (1992) 3 An. L.T.733.

CHAPTER II

HINDU MARRIAGES

5. Conditions for a Hindu marriage:- A marriage may be solemnized between any two Hindus, if the following conditions are fulfilled, namely;-
    (i)   neither party has a spouse living at the time of the marriage;
    (ii)   at the time of the marriage, neither party-
    (a)   is incapable of giving a valid consent to it in consequence of unsoundness of mind; or
    (b)   though capable of giving a valid consent, has been suffering from mental disorder of such a kind or to such an extent as to be unit for marriage and the procreation of children; or
    (c)   has been subject to recurrent attacks of insanity;
    (iii)   the bridegroom has completed the age of (twenty-one years) and the bride, the age of (eighteen years) at the time of the marriage;
    (iv)   in the parties are not within the degrees of prohibited relationship, unless the custom or usage governing each of them permits of a marriage between the two;
    (v)   the parties are not *sapindas* of each other, unless the custom or usage governing each of them permits of a marriage between the two;

---

2. Substituted by Act 68 of 1976, S.2, for Cl. (ii) (w.e.f.25-5-1976).

3. The words "or epilepsy" omitted by Act 39 of 1999, S.2 (w.e.f. 29-12-1999)

4. Substituted by Act 2 of 1978, S.6 and /sch., for "eighteen years" and "fifteen years", respectively (w.e.f.1-10-1978).

5. Cl. (vi) omitted by Act 2 of 1978, S.6 and Sch. (w.e.f.1-10-1978).

Objects and Reasons:- This section prescribed the essential requisites for a Hindu marriage, sub-clause (i) of which introduces monogamy. Sub-clauses (iv) and (v) require that the parties should not be within the degrees of prohibited relationship or be sapindas of each other unless in either case there is a custom or usage modifying that rule.

In sub-clause (vi), the amendment will ensure that until the bride attains majority, no marriage takes place without the consent of the guardian-in-marriage. Under the original Bill, consent of the guardian was required only if the girl was between the ages of 15 and 16, and once she attained her 16th year she could dispense with the consent of her guardian although she was still a minor.

COMMENTS

The concept of Hindu marriage under the Act is still a sacrament as envisaged under the Hindu Law. It cannot, therefore, be contracted by mere consent of the parties to it. A marriage to be valid under the Act must satisfy the conditions laid down in S.5 and should be solemnized as specified in S.7: Ravinder Kumar v. Kamal Kanta I.L.R (1973) Bom. 1220; 1973 Mah.L.J.310.

Hindu marriage if is to be solemnized under S.5 then both the parties of such marriage must be Hindua. As seen from sub-S, (3) of S.2 a person though not a Hindu by religion has to be regarded as Hindu and the Hindu Marriage Act applies to him because of sub-Ss. (1) and (2) of S.2 thereof. However, Hindu marriage could be solemnized in accordance with the customary rights and ceremonies of either party thereto as is envisaged in S.7; Jacintha Kamath v. K.Padmanabha Kamath A.I.R. 1992 Karn. 372 (1992) 2 Hindu L.R.114(D.B.)

A wife whose marriage has been declared null and void ipso jure under s.11 as envisaged under S.5(i), (iv), held, ceases to be a wife within the meaning of S.18 of the Hindu Adoptions and Maintenance act, 1956; she is not entitled to claim maintenance under the latter provision: Basappa v. Siddagangamma (1992) 2 Karn. L.J.357:I.L.R. (1992) Karn.1798.

The expression "incurably of sound mind", held, cannot be so widely interpreted as to cover the feeble minded or possessors of weak or dull intellects who are capable of understanding the nature and consequences of their acts or controlling themselves and their affairs and reactions in the normal way; S.5(ii) lay down that neither party to a marriage must be incapable of giving valid consent due to unsoundness of mind or should have been suffering from mental disorder; S.12(i)(b) enables the other party to avoid the marriage contravening such a condition; S.13(1)(iii) provides for divorce where the other party has, subsequent to the marriage, developed incurable unsoundness of mind: Parvati Mishra v. Jagadananda Mishra (1995) 1 D.M.C. 77 (Madh.Pra.).

The marriages solemnized in violation of S.5(iii) remains unaffected; neither the marriage is void nor voidable: Rabindra Prasad v. Sita Devi A.I.R. 1986 Pat.128.

6. **Guardianship in marriage:-** [Omitted by the child marriage Restraint (Amendment) Act, 1978 (2 of 1978), section 6 and Schedule (w.e.f.1-10-1978).]
7. **Ceremonies for a Hindu Marriage**:- (1) A Hindu marriage may be solemnized in accordance with the customary rites and ceremonies of either party thereto.

(2) Where such rites and ceremonies include the saptapadi (that is, the taking of seven steps by the bridegroom and the bride jointly before the scared fire), the marriage becomes complete and binding when the seventh step is taken.

COMMENTS

A marriage is not proved unless the essential ceremonies required for its solemnization are proved to have been performed: Kanwal ram v. Himachal Pradesh Administration A.I.R. 1966 S.C.614.

A valid marriage can be performed between a Sikh and a Hindu by anand karaj, or by saptapadi: Aswani Kumar v. asha Rani (1992) 1 Hindu L.R. 307 (P.&.H.)

Section 7-A

State Amendments-[Pondicherry]:- In its application to the Union territory of Pondicherry, after S.7, insert the following section, namely:-

"7-A. Special provision regarding suyamariythai and seethiruththa marriages.- (1) This section shall apply to any marriage between any two Hindus, whether called suyamariythai marriage or seethiruththa marriage or by any other name, solemnized in the presence of relatives, friends or other persons-

  (a)   by each party to the marriage declaring in any language (which is understood by the parties and by at least two persons in whose presence the marriage is solemnized), that each takes the other to be his wife or, as the case may be, her husband; or
  (b)   by each party to the marriage garlanding the other or putting a ring upon any finger of the other; or
  (c)   by the tying of the thali.

(2)(a) Notwithstanding anything contained in section 7, but subject to the other provisions of this Act, all marriages to which the section applies solemnized after the commencement of the Hindu Marriage (Pondicherry Amendment) Act, 1971, shall be good and valid in law.

(b) Notwithstanding anything contained in section 7 or in any text, rule or interpretation of Hindu Law or any custom or usage as part of that law in force immediately before the commencement of the Hindu Marriage (Pondicherry Amendment) Act, 1971, or in any other in force immediately before such commencement or in any judgement, decree or order of any Court, but subject to sub-section (3), all marriages to which this section applies solemnized at any time before such commencement shall be deemed to have been, with effect on and from the date of the solemnization of each such marriage respectively, good and valid in law.

(3) Nothing contained in this section shall be deemed to-

  (a) render valid any marriage referred to in clause (b) of sub-section (2), if before the commencement of the Hindu Marriage (Pondicherry Amendment) act, 1971,-
  (i) such marriage has been dissolved under any custom or law; or

(ii) the woman who was a party to such marriage has, whether during or after the life of the other party thereto, lawfully married another, or

(b) render valid a marriage between any two Hindus solemnized at any time before such commencement, if such marriage was valid at that time; or

(c) render valid a marriage between any two Hindus solemnized at any time before such commencement, if such marriage was valid at that time on any ground other than that it was not solemnized in accordance with the customary rites and ceremonies of either party thereto:

Provided that nothing contained in the sub-section shall render any person liable to any punishment whatsoever by reason of anything done or omitted to be done by him before such commencement.

(4) Any child of the parties to a marriage referred to in clause (b) of sub-section (2) born of such marriage shall be deemed to their legitimate child:

Provided that in case falling under sub-clause (i) or, sub-clause(ii) of clause (a) of sub-section (3), such child was begotten before the date of the dissolution of the marriage or, as the case may be, before the date of the second of the marriages referred to in the said sub-clause (ii)-Pondicherry Act 14 of 1971, S.2 (w.e.f.9-7-1971).

[Tamil Nadu]:- In its application to the State of Tamil Nadu, after S.7, insert the following section, namely:-

"7-A. Special provision regarding suyamariythai and seethiruththa marriages.- (1) This section shall apply to any marriage between any two Hindus, whether called suyamariythai marriage or seethiruththa marriage or by any other name, solemnized in the presence of relatives, friends or other persons-
(a) by each party to the marriage declaring in any language (which is understood by the parties and by at least two persons in whose presence the marriage is solemnized), that each takes the other to be his wife or, as the case may be, her husband; or

(b) by each party to the marriage garlanding the other or putting a ring upon any finger of the other; or

(c)by the tying of the thali.

(2)(a) Notwithstanding anything contained in section 7, but subject to the other provisions of this Act, all marriages to which the section applies solemnized after the commencement of the Hindu Marriage (Madras Amendment) Act, 1967, shall be good and valid in law.

(b) Notwithstanding anything contained in section 7 or in any text, rule or interpretation of Hindu Law or any custom or usage as part of that law in force immediately before the commencement of the Hindu Marriage (Madras Amendment) Act, 1967, or in any other in force immediately before such commencement or in any judgement, decree or order of any Court, but subject to sub-section (3), all marriages to which this section applies solemnized at any time before such commencement shall be deemed to have been, with effect on and from the date of the solemnization of each such marriage respectively, good and valid in law.

(3) Nothing contained in this section shall be deemed to-

    (a) render valid any marriage referred to in clause (b) of sub-section (2), if before the commencement of the Hindu Marriage (Madras Amendment) act, 1967,-

(i) such marriage has been dissolved under any custom or law; or

(ii) the woman who was a party to such marriage has, whether during or after the life of the other party thereto, lawfully married another, or

    (b) render valid a marriage between any two Hindus solemnized at any time before such commencement, if such marriage was valid at that time; or

    (c) render valid a marriage between any two Hindus solemnized at any time before such commencement, if such marriage was valid at that time on any ground other than that it was not solemnized in accordance with the customary rites and ceremonies of either party thereto:

Provided that nothing contained in the sub-section shall render any person liable to any punishment whatsoever by reason of anything done or omitted to be done by him before such commencement.

(4) Any child of the parties to a marriage referred to in clause (b) of sub-section (2) born of such marriage shall be deemed to their legitimate child:

Provided that in case falling under sub-clause (i) or, sub-clause (ii) of clause (a) of sub-section (3), such child was begotten before the date of the dissolution of the marriage or, as the case may be, before the date of the second of the marriages referred to in the said sub-clause (ii)-Pondicherry Act 21 of 1967, S.2 (w.e.f.20-01-1968).

    8. Registration of Hindu marriages:- (1) For the purpose of facilitating the proof of Hindu marriages, the State Government may make rules providing that the parties to any such marriage may have the particulars relating to their marriage entered in such manner and subject to such conditions as may be prescribed in a Hindu Marriage Register kept for the purpose.

----

6. see the Hindu Marriage (Mysore) Rules, 1966, the Hindu Marriage Registration (Tamil Nadu) Rules, 1967; the Madhya Pradesh Hindu Marriage (Registration) Rules, 1956; the Pondicherry Hindu Marriage (Registration) Rules, 1969 and the Hindu Marriage Registration (Sikkim) Rules, 1991.

----

(2) Notwithstanding anything contained in sub-section (1), the State Government may, if it is of opinion that it is necessary or expedient so to do, provide that the entering of the particulars referred to in sub-section (1) shall be compulsory in the State or in any part thereof, whether in all cases or in such cases as may be specified, and where any such

direction has been issued, any person contravening any rule made in this behalf shall be punishable with fine which may extend to twenty-five rupees.

(3) All rules made under this section shall be laid before the State Legislature, as soon as may be, after they are made.

(4) The Hindu Marriage Register shall at all reasonable times be open for inspection, and shall be admissible as evidence of the statements therein contained and certified extracts therefrom shall, on application, be given by the Registrar on payment of the prescribed fee.

(5) Notwithstanding anything contained in this section, the validity of any Hindu marriage shall in no way be affected by the omission to make the entry.

COMMENTS

Merely because a marriage between the parties has been registered under S.8, held, that does not *ipso facto* imply the existence of a complete and lawful marriage between the parties: Krishan Paul v. Ashok Kumar Pal 1982 Hindu L.R.478: (1981-1982) 86 Cal.W.N.1088.

CHAPTER III
RESTITUTION OF CONJUGAL RIGHTS AND JUDICIAL SEPARATION

9. **Restitution of conjugal rights**:- 7[*] When either the husband or the wife has, without reasonable excuse, withdrawn from the society of the other, the aggrieved party may apply, by petition to the district Court, for restitution of conjugal rights and the Court, on being satisfied of the truth of the statements made in such petition and that there is no legal ground why the application should not be granted, may decree restitution of conjugal rights accordingly.
8[*Explanation*:- Where a question arises whether there has been reasonable excuse for withdrawal from the society, the burden of proving reasonable excuse shall be on the person who has withdrawn from the society.]
9[***]

Objects and Reasons-Clause 3:- Sub-clause (a) seeks to insert a new Explanation in sub-section (1) of section 9 to clarify that the burden of proving reasonable excuse for withdrawing from the society shall be on the person who has withdrawn from the society of other.

Sub-clause (b) seeks to omit sub-section (2) of section 9 as it has the unintended effect of restricting the scope of defense of reasonable excuse available to the respondent.

COMMENTS

S.9 is not violative of Art. 19(1)(g) of the Constitution: Sumitra Devi v. Narender Singh (1993-1) 103 Punj.L.R.422(F.B.).

----

7. The brackets and figure "(1)" omitted by Act 68 of 1976, S.3 (w.e.f.27-5-1976).
8. Added by Act 68 of 1976, S.3 (w.e.f.27-5-1976).

9. Sub-S. (2) Omitted by Act 68 of 1976, S.3(w.e.f.27-5-1976).

When the marriage is not one under the Hindu marriage Act, S.9 of the Act has no application: Chitralekha Shibu Kunju v. Shibu Kunju (1998) 2 D.M.C. 454 (Bom) (D.B.).

The words "reasonable excuse" should be understood in their ordinary meaning. It would be sufficient if the court is satisfied that there was reasonable cause for the objecting spouse to withdraw from the society of the petitioning spouse: Krishnamurthy v. Shymanthakamani (1976) 2 Karn.L.J. 361:1977 Hindu L.R.163 (D.B.).

When a petition under S.9 of the Hindu Marriage Act, 1955 is pending before the Family Court, S.24 of the 1955 Act can be invoked automatically for grant of interim maintenance, it is not necessary that there should be a separate provision for this purpose in the Family Courts Act, 1984: Vedantham v. Virmala (1990-1) 105 Mad.L.W.580: (1991)2 Hindu L.R.608.

The execution proceedings for a decree under S.9 conceives of only one contingency that if the decree is not obeyed, then the property of the opposite party can be attached; no force can be used to get the lady to the conjugal house: Vijay Kumar v. Neelam Rani A.I.R.2004 Raj. 256.

10. **Judicial separation**:- 10[(1) Either party to a marriage, whether solemnized before or after the commencement of this Act, may present a petition praying fr a decree for judicial separation on any of the grounds specified in sub-section (1) of section 13, and in the case of a wife also on any of the grounds specified in sub-section (2) thereof, as grounds on which a petition for divorce might have been presented.]
(2) Where a decree for judicial separation has been passed, it shall no longer be obligatory for the petitioner to cohabit with the respondent, but the Court may, on the application by petition of either party and on being satisfied of the truth of the statements made in such petition, rescind the decree if it considers it just and reasonable to do so.

Objects and reasons:- Section 10 deals with judicial separation and the main consequences which flow from a decree for judicial separation. A decree for judicial separation does not have the effect of terminating the marriage.

Joint Committee Report:- In considering this and the following clauses, the Joint Committee have taken into account the language employed and the scheme adopted in the Special Marriage Act, 1954, recently passed by the Parliament. In view, however, of the fact that Hindu Law has so far recognized polygamy, the Joint Committee feel that the approach to the problems of judicial separation and divorce need not necessarily be the same in both the cases and that it is neither necessary nor desirable in the present case that grounds for judicial separation and grounds for divorce should be identical as in the Special Marriage Act, 1954. Moreover, having regard to the high ideals which the Hindu Community has always lived up to, divorce should not be made easy and the law should be so framed as to provide the maximum opportunities for mutual adjustment. The scheme of this Bill is, therefore, slightly different. Apart from the changes in the language employed, the major changes made in clause 10 are,-

(a) "cruelty" is now a self-contained definition;

(b) One act of infidelity to the marriage tie now furnishes a ground for judicial separation instead of adultery as proposed in the original Bill; and

(c) The definition of "desertion" has been widened so as expressly to include willful neglect of the respondent.

COMMENTS

Judicial separation does not put an end to the marital status of the party: M.Narasimha Reddy v. M.Boosamma A.I.R. 1976. Andh. Pra. 77 (D.B.).

-

10. Substituted by Act 68 of 1976, S.4, for sub-S. (1) (w.e.f.27-5-1976).

-

If the Court comes to the conclusion that there are sufficient grounds to grant judicial separation, it shall grant judicial separation. If it finds that the grounds are not sufficient to grant judicial separation, it has to dismiss the petition for judicial separation. It is not legal for any Court to grant a decree for judicial separation only for a period of nine months or for any specified period: P.Kalyanasundaram v. K.Paquialatchamy A.I.R.2003 Mad.43 (D.B.).

S. 13-A contemplates giving an alternative relief only when the grounds mentioned in S.10 exist. Thus, where none of the grounds alleged for obtaining divorce had been established, held, no decree for judicial separation could be granted: Manthena Siromani v. M.Venkateswara Raju (1988) 2 Hindu L.R. 209 (Andh.Pra.) (D.B.).

CHAPTER IV
NULLITY OF MARRIAGE AND DIVORCE

11. Void marriages:- Any marriage solemnized after the commencement of this Act shall be null and void and may, on a petition presented by either party thereto, 11[against the other party], be so declared by a decree of nullity if it contravenes any one of the conditions specified I clauses (i), (iv) and (v) of section 5.

Objects and reasons:- Section 11 and 12 deal with cases where a marriage is null and void and cases where a marriage is voidable at the opinion of either party to the marriage. Until so avoided a voidable marriage should be regarded as good for all purposes. Where a marriage is a bigamous marriage or contravenes the rule relating to prohibited degrees, the marriage is regarded as null and void from the very beginning. In other cases the marriage is rendered voidable at the option of the parties as in many other systems of law.

COMMENTS

The marriage covered by S.11 are void *ipso jure*, that is, void from the very inception and have to be ignored as not existing in law at all if and when such a question arises. Although the section permits a formal declaration to be made on the presentation of a petition, it is not essential to obtain in advance such a formal declaration from a Court in a proceeding specifically commenced for the purpose. A marriage in contravention of S.11 must be treated as null and void from its very inception. Yamunabai Anantrao Adhav v. Anantrao Shivram Adhav A.I.R. 1988 S.C.644.

A wife whose marriage has been declared null and void *ipso jure* under S.11 an envisaged under Cl. (i), (iv) of Cl. (v) of S.5, held,ceases to be a wife within the meaning of S.18 of the Hindu Adoption and Maintenance Act, 1956; she is not entitled to claim maintenance under the latter provision: Basappa v. siddagangamma (1992) 2 Karn.L.J. 357: I.L.R. (1992) Karn. 1798.

12. Voidable marriages:- (1) Any marriage solemnized, whether before or after the commencement of this Act, shall be voidable and may be annulled by a decree of nullity on any of the following grounds, namely:-

12[(a) that the marriage has not been consummated owing to the impotence of the respondent; or]

(b) that the marriage is in contravention of the condition specified in clause (ii) of section 5; or

(c) that the consent of the petitioner, or where the consent of the guardian in marriage of the guardian in marriage of the petitioner 13[was required under section 5, as it stood immediately before the commencement of the Child Marriage Restraint (Amendment) Act, 1978], the consent of such guardian was obtained by force

----
----

11. Inserted by Act 68 of 1976, S.5 (w.e.f.27-5-1976)
12. Substituted by Act 68 of 1976, S.6 for Cl. (a) (w.e.f.27-5-1976).
13. Substituted by Act 2 of 1978, S.6 and Sch., for "is required under section 5" (w.e.f.1-10-1978).

14[or by fraud as to the nature of the ceremony or as to any material fact or circumstance concerning the respondent]; or

    (d) that the respondent was at the time of the marriage pregnant by some person other than the petitioner.

(2) Notwithstanding anything contained in sub-section (1), no petition for annulling a marriage-

    (a) on the ground specified in clause (c) of sub-section (1), shall be entertained if-
(i) the petition is presented more than one year after the force had ceased to operate or, as the case may be, the fraud had been discovered; or
(ii) the petitioner has, with his or her full consent, lived with the other party to the marriage as husband or wife after the force had ceased to operate or, as the case may be, the fraud had been discovered;

    (b) on the ground specified in clause (d) of sub-section (1), shall be entertained unless the Court is satisfied-
(i) that the petitioner was at the time of the marriage ignorant of the facts alleged;
(ii) that the proceedings have been instituted in the case of a marriage solemnized before the commencement of this Act within one year of such commencement and in the case of marriages solemnized after such commencement within one year from the date of marriage; and
(iii) that marital intercourse with the consent of the petitioner has not taken place since the discovery by the petitioner of the existence of 15 [the said ground].

COMMENTS

The bar contained in S.14 regarding filing of petition before one year from date of marriage does not apply to the petition for annulment of marriage: Smritikana Bag v. Dilip Kumar Bag A.I.R. 1982 Cal.547.

"Impotent" means a practical impossibility to perform sexual act in complete and perfect manner. Full and complete sexual penetration is an essential ingredient for ordinary and complete intercourse. However, the degree of sexual satisfaction obtained by the parties is irrelevant: Gayatri Bai v. Pradeep Kumar chaurasia (1998) 2 D.M.C. 211 (Madh.Pra.).

The word "fraud" within the meaning of S.12(1)(c) is not each and every misrepresentation or concealment, which may be fraudulent. The word "fraud" in the section has a limited meaning. In the section "fraud" refs to and refers only to the consent of the petitioner to the solemnization of the marriage. Therefore, (1) fraud within the meaning of S.12(1)(c) means either (a) deception as to the identity of the other party to the marriage, or (b) deception as to the nature of the ceremonies being performed; (2) where consent is given with the intention to marry the other party and with the knowledge that what is being solemnized is marriage, an objection to the validity of the marriage on the ground of any fraudulent misrepresentation or concealment is not tenable. Thus, mere concealment of the fact that the husband had been once married to another woman could not be a ground for annulment of marriage under S.12(1)(c): Rajaram Vishwakarma v. Deepabai A.I.R. 1974 Madh. Pra. 52.

13. Divorce:- (1) Any marriage solemnized, whether before or after the commencement of this Act, may, on a petition presented by either the husband or the wife, be dissolved by a decree of divorce on the ground that the other party-

----
----

14. Substituted by Act 68 of 1976, S.6, for "or fraud" (w.e.f.27-5-1976).
15. Substituted by Act 68 of 1976, S.6, for "the grounds for a decree" (w.e.f.27-5-1976).

[(i) has, after the solemnization of the marriage, had voluntary sexual intercourse with any person other than his or her spouse; or
(i-a) has, after the solemnization of the marriage, treated the petitioner with cruelty; or
(i-b) has deserted the petitioner for a continuo's period of not less than two years immediately preceding the presentation of the petition; or]
(ii) has ceased to be a Hindu by conversion to another religion; or
(iii) has been incurably of unsound mine, or has been suffering continuously or intermittently from mental disorder of such a kind and to such an extent that the petitioner cannot reasonably be expected to live with the respondent.
Explanation:- In this clause,-
  (a) the expression "mental disorder" means mental illness, arrested or incomplete development of mind, psychopathic, disorder or any other disorder or disability of mind and includes schizophrenia;
  (b) the expression "psychopathic disorder" means a persistent disorder or disability of mind (whether or not including sub-normality of intelligence) which results in abnormally aggressive or seriously irresponsible conduct on the part of the other party, and whether or not it requires or is susceptible to medical treatment; or]
(iv) has been suffering from a virulent and incurable form of leprosy; or
(v) has been suffering from venereal disease in a communicable form; or
(vi) has renounced the world by entering any religious order; or
(vii) has not been heard of as being alive for a period of seven years or more by those persons who would naturally have heard of it, had that party been alive;
[Explanation.- In this sub-section, the expression "desertion" means the desertion of the petitioner by the other party to the marriage without reasonable cause and without the consent or against the wish of such party, and includes the willful neglect of the petitioner by the other party to the marriage, and its grammatical variations and cognate expressions shall be construed accordingly.]

[1-A) Either party to a marriage, whether solemnized before or after the commencement of this Act, may also present a petition for the dissolution of the marriage by a decree of divorce on the ground-

(i) that there has been no resumption of cohabitation as between the parties to the marriage for a period of [one year] or upwards after the passing of a decree for judicial separation in a proceeding to which they were parties; or

----
----

16. Substituted by Act 68 of 1976, S.7, for Cl. (i) (w.e.f.27-5-1976)
17. Substituted by Act 68 of 1976, S.7, for Cl. (iii) (w.e.f.27-5-1976)
18. The words "for a period of not less than three years immediately preceding the presentation of the petition" omitted by Act 68 of 1976, S.7 (w.e.f.27-5-1976).
19. The word "or" omitted by Act 44 of 1964, S.2.
20. Inserted by Act 68 of 1976, S.7 (w.e.f.27-5-1976).
21. Cls. (viii) and (ix) omitted by Act 44 of 1964, S.2.
22. Inserted by Act 44 of 1964, S.2.
23. Substituted by Act 68 of 1976, S.7, for "two years" (w.e.f.27-5-1976).

(ii) that there has been no restitution of conjugal rights as between the parties to the marriage for a period of [one year] or upwards after the passing of a decree for restitution of conjugal rights in a proceeding to which they were parties.]
(2) A wife may also present a petition for the dissolution of her marriage by a decree of divorce on the ground,-
(i) in the case of any marriage solemnized before the commencement of this Act, that the husband had married again before such commencement or that any other wife of the husband married before such commencement was alive at the time of the solemnization of the marriage of the petitioner:
Provide that in either case the other wife is alive at the time of the presentation of the petition; or
(ii) that the husband has, since the solemnization of the marriage, been guilty of rape, sodomy or [bestiality; or]
[(iii) that in a suit under section 18 of the Hindu Adoption and Maintenance Act, 1956 (78 of 1956), or in a proceeding under section 125 of the code of Criminal Procedure, 1973 (2 of 1974) (or under the corresponding section 488 of the Code of the Criminal Procedure, 1898 (5 of 1898)), a decree or order, as the case may be, has been passed against the husband awarding maintenance to the wife notwithstanding that she was living apart and that since the passing of such decree or order, cohabitation between the parties has not been resumed for one year or upwards; or
(iv) that her marriage (whether consummated or not) was solemnized before she attained the age of fifteen years and she has repudiated the marriage after attaining that age but before attaining the age of eighteen years.
Explanation.- This clause applies whether the marriage was solemnized before or after the commencement of the Marriage Laws (Amendment) Act, 1976.]
Object and Reasons:- Section 13 specifies the grounds on which a decree for divorce may be obtained by either party to the marriage. In particular, a decree of divorce may be obtained if there is no reconciliation between the parties within a specified period after the passing of a decree for judicial separation or if a decree for restitution of conjugal rights is not complied with within a special period.
Section 13(1)(ii), read with section 23(1)(a).- A change in religion is not inconsistent with the continuance of conjugal love and it should, therefore, not be permissible for a party to the marriage to get a divorce by changing his or her religion. The right to get a divorce under this law is, therefore, given to the party who continues to

be a Hindu..... a somewhat similar right is given to a person changing his religion to Christianity under the converts' Marriage Dissolution Act, 1866.

State Amendment-[Uttar Pradesh].- In its application to Hindus domiciled in Uttar Pradesh and also when either party to the marriage was not at the time of marriage a Hindu domiciled in Uttar Pradesh, in S.13-

(i) in sub-S. (1), after Cl. (i), insert (and shall be deemed always to have been inserted) the following, namely:-

"(1-a) has persistently or repeatedly treated the petitioner with such cruelty as to cause a reasonable apprehension in the mind of the petitioner that it will be harmful or injurious for the petitioner to live with the other party, or", and

----
----

24. Substituted by Act 68 of 1976, S.7, for "two years" (w.e.f.27-5-1976).

25. Substituted by Act 68 of 1976, S.7, for "bestiality" (w.e.f.27-5-1976).

26. Inserted by Act 68 of 1976, S.7 (w.e.f.27-5-1976).

(ii) for Cl. (viii) (since repealed,) substitute (and shall be deemed always to have been so substituted) the following, namely:-

"(viii) has not resumed cohabitation after the passing of a decree for judicial separation against that party and-

    (a) a period of two years has elapsed since the passing of such decree, or

    (b) the case is one of exceptional hardship to the petitioner or of exceptional depravity on the part of other party; or"- Uttar Pradesh Act 13 of 1962, S.2 (w.e.f.7-11-1962).

COMMENTS

Irretrievable break down of marriage is not a ground recognized by law for grant of decree of divorce: Sudhir Singhal v. Neeta Singhal A.I.R.2001 Del.116.

The expression "cruelty" as envisaged under S.13 clearly admits in its ambit and scope such acts which may even cause mental agony to aggrieved party. Cruelty may result where the complaining spouse establishes his being treated with cruelty whether physical, mental, social or otherwise but the acts complained of must be more serious than ordinary wear and tear of marriage falling in the category of conscious acts cruel in nature as that is the underlying requirement of the provision: Neelu Kohli v. Naveen Kohli A.I.R.2004 All.1.

Mental cruelty in S.13(1)(i-a) can broadly be defined as that conduct which inflicts upon the other party such mental pain and suffering as would make it not possible for that party to live with the other. In other words, mental cruelty must be of such a nature that the parties cannot reasonably be expected to live together. V.Bhagat v. D.Bhagat (Mrs.) A.I.R. 1994 S.C.710: (1994) S.C.C. 337; Neelu Kohli v. Naveen Kohli A.I.R.2004 All.1.

Leveling of disgusting allegations of unchastity and indecent familiarity of wife with different persons outside wedlock and her having extra-marital relations with other persons, themselves will amount to cruelty: Jai Dayal v. Shakunthal Devi A.I.R.2004 Del.39.

The fact that wife was pregnant from some other person at the time of marriage would amount to cruelty and mental agony to the husband: Pawan Kumar v. Mukesh Kumari A.I.R. 2001 Raj.1.

A Hindu marriage solemnized under the Act can only be dissolved on any of the grounds specified under the Act: Sarla Mudgal President, Kalyani v. Union of India 1995 D.N.J 252: (1995) 2 D.M.C. 351 (S.C.).

Grounds of divorce are to be construed liberally: Reynold Rajamani v. Union of India A.I.R. 1982 S.C. 1261: (1982) 2 S.C.C. 474.

After the amendment of S.13 by the Marriage Laws (Amendment) Act, 1976, the proof of only one instance of voluntary sexual intercourse by the other party with any other person except his or her spouse, is enough for a decree of dissolution of marriage: Sanjukta Padhan v. Laxminarayan Padhan A.I.R. 1991 Ori.39; Rajendra Agrawal v. Sharda Devi A.I.R.1993 Madh. Pra. 142; Gali Kondaiah v. Gali Ankamma A.I.R. 1988 Andh. Pra. 68 (D.B.).

The burden to prove the adultery is on the peson who seeks dissolution of marriage on the ground of adultery: A.Hemamalini v. A.Pankajanaban (1995) 1 D.M.C. 258: (1994) 2 Hindu L.R. 671 (Andh. Pra.) (D.B.).

It is quite possible that a particular conduct may amount to "cruelty" in one case but the same conduct necessarily may not amount to "cruelty" due to change of various factors, in different set of circumstances. Therefore, it is essential for the petitioner, who claims relief, to prove that a particular/part of conduct or behaviour resulted in "cruelty" to him. No prior assumptions can be made in such matters: Naval Kishore Somani v. Poonam Somani A.I.R. 1999 Andh. Pra. 1 (D.B.).

Even a single act of violence which is of grievous and inexcusable in nature satisfies the test of cruelty: Mohanan v. Thankamani (1995) 1 D.M.C. 327; (1995) 2 Hindu L.R. 174 (Ker.) (D.B.); Sulekha Bairagi v. Kamala Kanta Bairagi A.I.R. 1980 Cal. 370 (D.B.).

"cruelty" under the Act can be both mental and physical. The degree of "cruelty" necessary to claim a matrimonial relief has not been defined under the Act. It depends from case to case and the Legislature has also refrained from giving a comprehensive definition of the expression that may cover all cases. In order to claim divorce on the ground of cruelty, it may be shown that the other spouse has treated the complaining spouse with cruelty which may be physical mental: Praveen Mehta v. Inderjeet Mehta (2002) 5 S.S.C.C. 706; A.I.R.2002 S.C.2582. Besides mental cruelty is a state of mind and feeling of one of the spouses due to the behaviour or behavioural pattern of the other. It is a matter of inference to be drawn from the facts and circumstances of the case and proper approach requires the assessment of the cumulative effect of the attending facts, and circumstances as established from the facts and circumstances on record. Physical cruelty on the other hand consists of such acts which endanger a physical health of one of the parties to the marriage and includes the inflicting bodily injury or giving cause for such injuries: Savitri Pandey v. Preme Chandra (2002) 2 S.C.C. 73: A.I.R. 2002 S.C. 591; Neelam Kumari v. Gurnam Singh A.I.R. 2004 P. & H.9.

The decisions of various Courts in India including the Supreme Court lead to the conclusion that a decree for divorce in terms of S.13(1)(iii) of the Act can be granted in the event the unsoundness of mind is held to be not curable. A party may behave strangely or oddly inappropriate and be progressive in deterioration in the level of work which may lead to a conclusion that he or she suffers from an illness of slow growing developing over the years. The disease, however, must be of such a kind that the other spouse cannot reasonably be expected to live with him or her. A few strong instances indicating short temper and somewhat erratic behaviour on the part of the spouse may not amount to his/her suffering continuously or intermittently from mental disorder: Sharda v. Dharmapal (2003) 4 S.C.C.493.

A matrimonial Court has the power to order a person to undergo medical test. Passing of such an order by the Court would not be in violation of the right to personal liberty under Art. 21. However, the court should exercise such a power if the applicant has a strong prima facie case ands there is sufficient material before the court. If despite the order of the Court the respondent refuses to submit himself to medical examination, the Court will be entitled to draw and adverse inference against him: Sharda v. Dharmapal (2003) 4 S.C.C.493.

Desertion implies not only the factum of separation but also the intention to separate permanently and put an end to the matrimonial relationship and cohabitation; there can be no desertion without animus deserendi or if the husband himself is responsible for the wife living away from the husband or if the wife has sufficient reason to live away from the husband: Saroja v. Arumugam (1989-1) 103 Mad. L.W.116(1989) 1 Hindu L.R.528.

The onus of proving that the other spouse is of incurably unsound mind or is suffering from mental disorder, held, lies on the party alleging it; it must be proved by cogent and clear evidence: Parvati Mishra v. Jagadananda (1995) 1 D.M.C. 77 (Madh.Pra.).

For the success of a petition under S.13(2)(iv), the petitioner has to prove three things; (a) that her marriage was solemnized before she attained the age of 15 years; (b) that she repudiated the marriage after attaining the age of 18 years; and (c) that she repudiated the marriage before attaining the age of 18 years. Whether the marriage was consummated or not is immaterial and beside the point. It is also immaterial whether the repudiation was made before the Marriage Laws (Amendment) Act, 1976 came into force or thereafter. Even if the repudiation was made before coming into force of the Amending Act, the wife can take advantage of this provision in such a petition and can be granted a decree for divorce under S.13(2)(iv) of the Act: Raju v. Ratan (1988) 2 Hindu L.R.257(Raj.).

[13-A. Alternate relief in divorce proceedings.- In any proceeding under this Act, on a petition for dissolution of marriage by a decree of divorce, except in so far as the petition is founded on the grounds mentioned in clauses (ii), (vi) and (vii) of sub-section (1) of section 13, the Court may, if it considers it just so to do having regard to the circumstances of the case, pass instead a decree for judicial separation.

COMMENTS

The Court is not competent to grant the relief of judicial separation under S.13-A, when the petitioner had prayed for relief under S.13(1)(ia) and (ib) but failed to prove: Vijayalakshmi Balasubramanian v. R.Balasubramaniam (1998) 1 D.M.C. 210 (Mad.) (D.B.).

----

27. Ss.13-A and 13-B inserted by Act 68 of 1976, S.8 (w.e.f. 27-5-1976).

-----------13-B. Divorce Mutual consent.- (1) Subject to the provisions of this Act a petition for dissolution of marriage by a decree of divorce may be presented to the district Court by both the parties to a marriage together, whether such marriage was solemnized before or after the commencement of the Marriage Laws (Amendment) Act, 1976, on the ground that they have been living separately for a period of one year or more, that they have not been able to live together and that they have mutually agreed that the marriage should be dissolved.

(2) On the motion of both the parties made not earlier that six months after the date of the presentation of the petition referred to in sub-section (1) and not later than eighteen

months after the said date, if the petition is not withdrawn in the meantime, the court shall, on being satisfied, after hearing the parties and after making such inquiry as it thinks fit, that a marriage has been solemnized and that the averments in the petition are true, pass a decree of divorce declaring the marriage to be dissolved with effect from the date of the decree.]

COMMENTS

A petition under S.13-B is not entertainable by the Appellate Court; it has to be filed in the original Court: N.Vijaya Raghavan v. K.Sharda A.I.R. 2001 Karn.300 (D.B.).

No decree can be passed otherwise than under section 13-B for divorce on the basis of compromise: Munesh v. Anasuyamma A.I.R. 2001 Karn.355 (D.B.).

A decree of divorce by mutual consent can be granted when and only when the Court is satisfied about (i) marriage having been solemnized between the parties; (ii) the parties have been living separately for more than a year before presenting the petition; (iii) they were not able to live together at the time of presenting the petition and continue to live apart; (iv) they had mutually agreed to dissolve the marriage before or at the time the petition was presented; and (v) the averments made in the petition are true and conditions under S.23 are fulfilled. Thus, the Court amongst other factors has to exclude the possibility of the consent of other party being obtained by force, fraud or undue influence, and also see through if there is any collusion: Krishna Khetarpal v. Satish Lal A.I.R. 1987 P. & H.19].

There cannot be any written agreement between husband and wife for divorce contrary to the provisions contained in Hindu Marriage Act, both spouses being Hindus: Malayaiah v. G.S.Vasatha Lakshmi (1997) 2 D.M.C. 88 (Karn).

14. No petition for divorce to be presented within one year of marriage:- (1) Notwithstanding anything contained in this Act, it shall not be competent for any Court to entertain any petition for dissolution of a marriage by a decree of divorce, {unless at the date of the presentation of the petition one year has elapsed} since the date of the marriage:

Provided tat the Court may, upon application made to it in accordance with such rules as may be made by the High Court in that behalf, allow a petition to be presented {before one year has elapsed} since the date of the marriage on the ground that the case is one of exceptional hardship to the petitioner or of exceptional depravity on the part of the respondent, but, if it appears to the Court at the hearing of the petition that the petitioner obtained leave to present the petition by any misrepresentation or concealment of the nature of the case, the Court may, if it pronounces a decree, do so subject to the condition that the decree shall not have effect until after

---

28. Substituted by Act 68 of 1976, S.9, for "unless at the date of the presentation of the petition three years have elapsed" (w.e.f.27-5-1976).
29. Substituted by Act 68 of 1976, S.9, for "before three years have elapsed" (w.e.f.27-5-1976).

---

the [expiry of one year] from the date of the marriage or may dismiss the petition without prejudice to any petition which may be brought after the [expiration of the said one year] upon the same or substantially the same facts as those alleged in support of the petition so dismissed.

(2) In disposing of any application under this section for leave to present a petition for divorce before the [expiration of one year] from the date of the marriage, the Court shall have regard to the interests of any children of the marriage and to the question whether there is a reasonable probability of a reconciliation between the parties before the expiration of the [said one year].

15. Divorced persons when may marry again.- When a marriage has been dissolved by a decree of divorce and either there is no right of appeal against the decree or, if there is such a right of appeal, the time for appealing has expired without an appeal having been presented or an appeal has been presented but has been dismissed, it shall be lawful for either party to the marriage to marry again:

16. Legitimacy of children of void and viodable marriages:- (1) Notwithstanding that a marriage is null and void under section 11, any child of such marriage who would have been legitimate if the marriage had been valid, shall be legitimate, whether such child is born before or after the commencement of the Marriage Laws (Amendment) act, 1976, and whether or not a decree of nullity is granted in respect of that marriage under this Act and whether or not the marriage is held to be void otherwise than on a petition under this Act.

(2) Where a decree of nullity is granted in respect of a voidable marriage under section 12, any child begotten or conceived before the decree is made, who would have been the legitimate child of the parties to the marriage if at the date of the decree it had been dissolved instead of being annulled, shall be deemed to be their legitimate child notwithstanding the decree of nullity.

(3) Nothing contained in sub-section (1) or sub-section (2) shall be construed as conferring upon any child of a marriage which is null and void or which is annulled by a decree of nullity under section, 12, any rights in or to the property of any person, other than the parents, in any case where, but for the passing of this Act, such child would have been incapable of possessing or acquiring any such rights by reason of his not being the legitimate child of his parents.]

COMMENTS

S.16 Intends to bring about social reforms, conferment of social status of legitimacy on a group of innocent children, otherwise treated as bastards, is its prime object: Parayan Kandiyal Eravath Kanapravan Kalliani Amma v. K.Devi J.T. (1996) 4 S.C. 656.

Children born of viod or viodable marriage, held, not entitled to claim inheritance in ancestral coparcenary property but entitled to claim inheritance in property of parents: Jinia Keotin v. Sitaram Manjhi (2003) 1 S.C.C. 730.

----

30. Substituted by Act 68 of 1976, S.9, for "expiry of three years" (w.e.f.27-5-1976).
31. Substituted by Act 68 of 1976, S.9, for "expiration of the said three years" (w.e.f.27-5-1976).
32. Substituted by Act 68 of 1976, S.9, for "expiration of three years" (w.e.f.27-5-1976).
33. Substituted by Act 68 of 1976, S.9, for "said three years" (w.e.f.27-5-1976).
34. Proviso omitted by Act 68 of 1976, S.10 (w.e.f.27-5-1976).
35. Substituted by Act 68 of 1976, S.11 (w.e.f.27-5-1976).

----

17. Punishment of bigamy:- Any marriage between two Hindus solemnized after the commencement of this Act is void if at the date of such marriage either party had a husband or wife living; and the provisions of sections 494 and 495 of the Indian Penal code (45 of 1860) shall apply accordingly.

COMMENTS

S.17 of the Hindu Marriage Act which makes bigamy punishable is not ultra vires Art 21 of the Constitution: Chander Pal v. Kehsv Deo (1989) 2 Hindu L.R.11 (All.) (D.B.).

18. Punishment for contravention of certain other conditions for a Hindu marriage:- Every person who procures a marriage of himself or herself to be solemnized under this Act in contravention of the conditions specified in clauses (iii), (iv), [and (v) of section 5 shall be punishable-

(a) in the case of contravention of the condition specified in clause (iii) of section 5, with rigorous imprisonment which may extend to two years or with fine which may extend to one lakh rupees, or with both;]

(b) in the case of contravention of the condition specified in clause (iv) or clause (v) of section 5, with simple imprisonment which may extend to one month, or with fine which may extend to one thousand rupees, or with both;

Joint Committee Report:- The Joint Committee are of the opinion that it is desirable to provide for the punishment of persons contravening the other important conditions for a Hindu marriage specified in clause 5 (section 5). Clause 17 (section 17) has already made provision for the punishment of bigamous marriages and this clause seeks to punish persons who contravene the conditions specified in sub-clauses (iii), (iv), (v) and (vi) (now omitted) of clause 5. In framing the punishment the Joint Committee have had in mind the gravity of the offence in each case and the punishment prescribed for certain similar offences in the Child Marriage Restraint Act, 1929.

CHAPTER V
JURISDICTION AND PROCEDURE

[19. Court to which petition shall be presented:- Every petition under this Act shall be presented to the district Court within the local limits of whose ordinary original civil jurisdiction-

(i) the marriage was solemnized, or

(ii) the respondent, at the time of the presentation of the petition, resides, or

(iii) the parties to the marriage last resided together, or

[(iii-a) in case the wife is the petitioner, where she is residing on the date of presentation of the petition, or]

(iv) the petitioner is residing at the time of the presentation of the petition, in a case where the respondent is, at that time, residing outside the territories to which this Act extends, or has not been heard of as being alive for a period of seven years or more by those persons who would naturally have heard of him if he were alive.]

----

36. Substituted by Act 2 of 1978, S.6 and Sch., for "(v) and (vi)" (w.e.f.1-10-1978).
36a. Substituted by the Prohibition of Child Marriage Act, 2006 (6 of 2007), S.20, for Cl. (a). Prior to its substitution, Cl. (a) in the case of a contravention of the condition

specified in clause (iii) of section 5, with simple imprisonment which may extend to fifteen days, or with fine which may extend to one thousand rupees, or with both;".
37. The word "and" omitted by Act 2 of 1978, S.6 and Sch. (w.e.f.1-10-1978).
38. Cl.(c) omitted by Act 2 of 1978, S.6 and Sch. (w.e.f.1-10-1978).
39. Substituted by Act 68 of 1976, S.12, for S.19 (w.e.f.27-5-1976).
40. Inserted by Act 50 of 2003, S.4 (w.e.f.23-12-2003).

----

20. Contents and verification of petitions:- (1) Every petition presented under this Act shall state as distinctly as the nature of the case permits the facts on which the claim to relief is founded [and, except in a petition under section 11, shall also sate] that there is no collusion between the petitioner and the other party to the marriage.

(2) The statements contained in every petition under this Act shall be verified by the petitioner or some other competent person in the manner required by law for the verification of plaints, and may, at the hearing, be referred to as evidence.

21. Application of Act 5 of 1908:- Subject to the other provisions contained in this Act and to such rules as the High Court may make in this behalf, all proceedings under this Act shall be regulated, as far as may be, by the Code of Civil Procedure, 1908 (5 of 1908).

COMMENTS

In view of S.21, the matrimonial proceedings before the District Courts are to be regulated by ordinary rules of procedure including those relating to the provisions for recording evidence contained in the Evidence Act. Thus, in accepting or rejecting a prayer for obtaining expert opinion regarding blood test, the Court would be generally guided by the principles embodied in S.45 of the Evidence Act: Kartick Chandra v. Sabita Das (1986) 2 Hindu L.R. 219 (D.B.).

[21-A. Power to transfer petition in certain cases.- (1) Where-
(a) a petition under this Act has been presented to a district Court having jurisdiction by a party to a marriage praying for a decree for judicial separation under section 10 or for a decree of divorce under section 13, and
(b) another petition under this Act has been presented thereafter by the other party to the marriage praying for a decree for judicial separation under section 10 or for a decree of divorce under section 13 on any ground, whether in the same district Court or in a different District Court, in the same State or in a different State,
the petitions shall be dealt with as specified in sub-section (2).
(2) IN a case where sub-section (1) applies,-
(a) if the petitions are presented to the same district court, both the petitions shall be tried and heard together by that district Court;
(b) if the petitions are presented to different district courts, the petition presented later shall be transferred to the district Court in which the earlier petition was presented and both the petitions shall be heard and disposed of together by the district Court in which the earlier petition was presented.
(3) In a case where clause (b) of sub-section (2) applies, the Court or the Government, as the case may be, competent under the Code of Civil Procedure, 1908 (5 of 1908), to transfer any suit or proceeding from the district Court in which the later petition has been presented to the district Court in which the earlier petition is pending,

shall exercise its powers to transfer such later petition as if it had been empowered so to do under the said Code.]

21-B. Special provision relating to trail and disposal of petition under the Act:-

(1) The trial of a petition under this Act shall, so far as is practicable consistently with the interest of justice in respect of the trial, be continued from day to day until its conclusion unless the court

----
----

41. Substituted by Act 68 of 1976, S.13, for "and shall also state" (w.e.f.27-5-1976).
42. Inserted by Act 68 of 1976, S.14 (w.e.f.27-5-1976).

Finds the adjournment of the trial beyond the following day to be necessary for reasons to be recorded.

(2) Every petition under this Act shall be tried as expeditiously as possible and endeavour shall be made to conclude the trial within six months from the date of service of notice of the petition on the respondent.

(3) Every appeal under this Act shall be heard as expeditiously as possible, and endeavour shall be made to conclude the hearing within three months from the date of service of notice of appeal on the respondent.]

[21-C. Documentary evidence:- Notwithstanding anything in any enactment to the contrary, no document shall be inadmissible in evidence in any proceeding at the trial of a petition under this Act on the ground that it is not duly stamped or registered.]

[22. Proceedings to be in camera and may not be printed or published:- (1) Every proceeding under this Act shall be conducted in camera and it shall not be lawful for any person to print or publish any matter in relation to any such proceeding except a judgment of the High Court of the Supreme Court printed or published with the previous permission of the Court.

(2) If any person prints or publishes any matter in contravention of the provisions contained in sub-section (1), he shall be punishable with fine which may extend to one thousand rupees.]

23. Decree in proceedings:- (1) In any proceeding under this Act, whether defended or not, if the Court is satisfied that-

(a) any of the grounds for granting relief exists and the petitioner [except in cases where the relief is sought by him on the ground specified in sub-clause (a), sub-clause (b) or sub-clause (c) of clause (ii) of section 5] is not in any way taking advantage of his or her own wrong or disability for the purpose or such relief, and

(b) where the ground of the petition is the ground specified in clause (i) of sub-section (1) of section 13, the petitioner has not in any manner been accessory to or connived at or condoned the act or acts complained of, or where the ground of the petition is cruelty the petitioner has not in any manner condoned the cruelty, and

(bb) when a divorce is sought on the ground of mutual consent, such consent has not been obtained by force, fraud or undue influence, and]

(c) [the petition (not being a petition presented under section 11) is not presented or prosecuted in collusion with the respondent, and

(d) There has not been any unnecessary or improper delay in instituting the proceeding, and

----
----

43. Inserted by Act 68 of 1976, S.14 (w.e.f.27-5-1976).
44. Substituted by Act 68 of 1976, s.15, for S.22 (w.e.f.27-5-1976).
45. Inserted by Act 68 of 1976, S.16 (w.e.f.27-5-1976).
46. The words, brackets and figures "in clause (f) of sub-section (1) of section 10, or" omitted by Act 68 of 1976, S.16 (w.e.f.27-5-1976).
47. Substituted by Act 68 of 1976, S.16, for "the petition" (w.e.f.27-5-1976).

(e) there is no other legal ground why relief should not be granted, then, and in such a case, but not otherwise, the court shall decree such relief accordingly.

(2) Before proceeding to grant any relief under this Act, it shall be the duty of the Court in the first instance, in every case where it is possible so to do consistently with the nature and circumstances of the case, to make every endeavour to bring about a reconciliation between the parties.

[Provided that nothing contained in this sub-section shall apply to any proceeding wherein relief is sought on any of the grounds specified in clause (ii), clause (iii), clause (iv), clause (v), clause (vi) of clause (vii) of sub-section (1) of section 13.]

(3) For the purpose of the aiding the Court in bringing about such reconciliation, the court may, if the parties so desire or if the Court thinks it just and proper so to do, adjourn the proceedings for a reasonable period not exceeding fifteen days and refer the matter to any person named by the parties in this behalf or to any person nominated by the Court if the parties fail to name any person, with directions to report to the Court, as to whether reconciliation can be and has been, effected and the Court shall in disposing of the proceeding have due regard to the report.

(4) In every case where a marriage is dissolved by a decree of divorce, the Court passing the decree shall give a copy thereof free of cost to each of the parties.]

COMMENTS

S.24 of the Act is not controlled by S.23: Gopal v. Dhapubai (1986) 2 Hindu L.R. 253 (Madh.Pra.).

[23-A. Relief for Respondent in divorce and other proceedings:- In any proceeding for divorce or judicial separation or resolution of conjugal rights, the respondent may not only oppose the relief sought on the ground of petitioner's adultery, cruelty or desertion, but also make a counter-claim for any relief under this Act on that ground; and if the petitioner's adultery, cruelty or desertion is proved, the Court may give to the respondent any relief under this Act to which he or she would have been entitled if he or she had presented a petition seeking such relief on that ground.]

24. Maintenance pendent elite and expenses of proceedings:- Where in any proceeding under this Act it appears to the Court that either the wife or the husband, as the case may be, has no independent income sufficient for her or his support and the necessary expenses of the proceeding, it may, on the application of the wife or the husband, order the respondent to pay to the petitioner the expenses of the proceeding, and monthly during the proceeding such sum as, having regard to the petitioner's own income and the income of the respondent, it may seem to the Court to be reasonable.

[Provide that the application for the payment of the expenses of the proceeding and such monthly sum during the proceeding, shall, as far as possible, be disposed of within sixty days from the date of service of notice on the wife or the husband, as the case may be.]

---

48. Added by Act 68 of 1976, S.16 (w.e.f.27-5-1976).
49. Inserted by Act 68 of 1976, S.16 (w.e.f.27-5-1976).
50. Inserted by Act 68 of 1976, S.17 (w.e.f.27-5-1976).
51. Inserted by Act 49 of 2001, S.8 (w.e.f.24-9-2001).

Objects and Reasons:- Sections 24 and 26 of the Hindu Marriage Act, 1955 do not contain any time-limit for disposal of applications for alimony pendente lite or the maintenance and education of minor children. More than 670 cases or understood to be pending in various High Courts under section 24 of the Hindu Marriage Act, 1955. As a part of the judicial reforms process, it is proposed to make necessary amendments in the enactments, i.e., sections 36 and 41 of the Indian Divorce Act, 1869, sections 39 and 49 of the Parsi Marriage and Divorce Act, 1936, sections 36 and 38 of the Special Marriage Act, 1954 and sections 24 and 26 of the Hindu Marriage Act, 1955 with a view to making provisions that an applications for alimony pendent elite or the maintenance and education of minor children shall be disposed of within sixty days from the date of service of notice on the respondent.

COMMENTS

Relevant consideration for grant of maintenance pendent elite is that the spouse seeking maintenance should not have independent income sufficient for her/his support-Once Court reaches its conclusion in that regard, it has to grant maintenance and only discretion left with the Court is with regard to quantum of maintenance: Amarjit Kaur v. Harbhajan Singh (2003) 10 S.C.C. 228

S.24 is enacted to provide relief by way of maintenance and litigation expenses to a spouse unable to maintain itself during the pendency of the proceedings; it is a benevolent provision: Lata v. Dhanpal (1995) 2 D.M.C. 440 (Madh. Pra).

Cases where the parties disclose their actual income are extremely rare. Experience, therefore, dictates that where a decision has to be taken pertaining to the claim for maintenance, the quantum to be granted, the safer and surer method to be employed for coming to a realistic conclusion is to look at the status of the parties, since whilst incomes can be concealed, the status is palpably evident to all concerned. If any opulent lifestyle is enjoyed by waring spouses, he should not be heard to complaint or plead that he has only a meager income: Radhika v. Vincent Rangta A.I.R.2004 Del 323.

The maintenance does not mean only the bare maintenance of food and clothing, but it does include the basic additional expenses for education of the child if the status of she father or the family is of such type: Remani Menon v. K.G. Omnakuttan A.I.R.2004 Guj.23.

The fact that there is a strong possibility of the marriage being declared as a nullity is no ground for declining even the basic right to claim interim alimony and expenses of the litigation: Sushila Viresh Chhadva v. Viresh Nagshi Chandra (1996) 1 Mah.L.J.288.

The doctrine of alimony in its strict sense means the allowance due to wife from husband; when the wife has no separate means sufficient for her defence and subsistence, she can claim for maintenance pendent elite. No distinction can be made between a case filed under S.12 and another filed under S.13 of the Hindu Marriage Act: Sandeep Kumar v. State of Jharkhand A.I.R. 2004 Jhar.22.

Question of maintenance pendent elite and litigation expenses arises with the filing of an application for matrimonial reliefs under the Hindu Marriage Act. It ends as the proceedings terminate. It has no separate existence and cannot stand by itself. No application for maintenance pendent elite or litigation expenses can exist independently unless lis is there: Ramactar Verma v. Chintamani A.I.R. 2004 Madh. Pra.137.

25. Permanent alimony and maintenance:- (1) Any Court exercising jurisdiction under this Act may, at the time of passing any decree or at any time subsequent thereto, on application made to it for the purpose by either the wife or the husband, as the case may be, order that the respondent shall, pay to the applicant for he or his maintenance and support such gross sum or such monthly or periodical sum for a term not exceeding the life of the applicant as, having regard to the respondent's own income and other property, if any, the income and other property of the applicant [the conduct of the parties and other circumstances of the case], it may seem to the

----
----

52. The words "while the applicant remains unmarried" omitted by Act 68 of 1976, S.18 (w.e.f.27-5-1976).
53. Substituted by Act 68 of 1976, S.18, for "and the conduct of the parties" (w.e.f.27-5-1976).

Court to be just, and any such payment may be secured, if necessary, by a charge on the immovable property of the respondent.
(2) If the Court is satisfied that there is a change in the circumstances of either party at any time after it has made an order under sub-section (1), it may, at the instance of either party, vary, modify or rescind any such order in such manner as the Court may deem just.
(3) If the Court is satisfied that the party in whose favour an order has been made under this section has remarried or, if such party is the wife, that she has not remained chaste, or, if such party is the husband, that he has had sexual intercourse with any woman outside wedlock, [it may at the instance of the other party vary, modify or rescind any such order in such manner as the Court may deem just.]

COMMENTS

The relief of permanent alimony cannot be given where the main petition for relief under the Act such as divorce, judicial separation, etc., is dismissed or withdrawn: Badri Prasad v. Urmila Mahobiya A.I.R. 2001 Madh.Prad. 106.

S.24 and S.25 are enacted with the object of removing the handicap of a wife or husband with no independent income sufficient for living or meeting litigation expenses; such a relief can be granted to the husband as well who may also be deprived of the same on proof of his having sexual intercourse outside the wedlock: Lalit Mohan v. Tripta Devi A.I.R.1990 J&K.7.

"Illegitimate wife" [or faithful mistress"] cannot be included in the word "wife" as contained in S.25 of the Hindu Marriage Act: Bhausaheb v. Leelabai A.I.R. 2004 Bom. 283 (F.B.)

Under S.25 of the Hindu Marriage Act, the Court is entitled to pass an order of alimony even when the original petition is dismissed. If the Court is competent to pass an order of alimony even at the time of dismissal of the petition, there is no reason why Court cannot grant an interim alimony during the pendency of the petition on the ground that the petitioner is not likely to succeed in the main petition: Mangilal S.Mundada v. Mangala M.Mundada A.I.R. 2004 Bom.266.

When the words of S.25 of the Hindu Marriage Act, 1955 are very much clear on the point that such application can be filed after passing of the decree, therefore, mere fact that the appeal is pending in higher Court would not effect the fate of the application, which was filed after passing of the decree: Surendra Kumar Bhansali v. Judge, Family Court A.I.R. 2004 Rsj.257.

The Court may grant permanent maintenance to a party while disposing of the main petition even if no proper application has been moved: Chandrika v. Vijayakumar (1996-1) 117 Mad. L.W. 695 (D.B.).

26. Custody of children:- In any proceeding under this Act, the Court may, from time to time, pass such interim orders and make such provisions in the decree as it may been just and proper with respect to the custody, maintenance and education of minor children, consistently with their wishes, wherever possible, and may, alter the decree, upon application by petition for the purpose, make from time to time, all such orders and provisions with respect to the custody, maintenance and education of such children as might have been made by such decree or interim orders in case the proceeding for obtaining such decree were still pending, and the Court may also from time to time revoke, suspend or vary any such orders and provisions previously made.

----
54. Substituted by Act 68 of 1976, s.18, for "it shall rescind the order: (w.e.f.27-5-1976).

[Provided that the application with respect to the maintenance and education of the minor children, pending the proceeding for obtaining such decree, shall, as far as possible, be disposed of within sixty days from the date of service of notice on the respondent.]

COMMENTS

S.26 enables the Court from time to time, to pass such interim order and make such provisions in a decree as it may deem just and proper with respect to the custody, maintenance and education of minor children. It enables the Court to do so, not only during the time the proceedings are pending but also after a decree has been passed in any proceedings under the Hindu Marriage Act: Vivek Yashavant Bhagwat v. Rekhs Vivek Bhagwat (1986) 1 Hindu L.R.46 (Madh.Pra.).

27. Disposal of property:- In any proceeding under this Act, the Court may make such provisions in the decree as it deems just and proper with respect to any property presented, at or about the time of marriage, which may belong jointly to both the husband and the wife.

COMMENTS

S.27 of the Act dealing with "disposal of property" is unambiguous and, therefore, marginal note of said section may not be used as an aid to its interpretation: Shakuntala v. Mahesh Atmaram Badlani A.I.R. 1989 Bom.353.

S.27 of the Hindu Marriage Act does not confine or restrict the jurisdiction of matrimonial Courts to deal only with the joint property of the parties, which is presented at or about the time of marriage but also permits disposal of exclusive property of the parties provided they were presented at or about the time of marriage: Hemant Kumar Agrahari v. Lakshmi Devi A.I.R.2004 All.126 (D.B.).

No order under S.27 can be passed with the respect to the property which exclusively belongs to the wife: Inderjit Singh v. Manjit Kaur (1987) 2 Hindu L.R.496(1988) 1 D.M.C. 129 (P.&H.).

28. Appeals from decrees and orders:- (1) All decrees made by the Court in any proceeding under this Act shall, subject to the provisions of sub-section (3), be appealable as decrees of the Court made in the exercise of its original civil jurisdiction, and every such appeal shall lie to the Court to which appeals ordinarily lie from the decisions of the Court given in the exercise of its original civil jurisdiction.

(2) Orders made by the Court in any proceeding under this Act under section 25 or section 26 shall, subject to the provisions of sub-section (3), be appealable if they are not interim orders, and every such appeal shall lie to the Court to which appeals ordinarily lie from the decisions of the Court given in exercise of its original civil jurisdiction.

(3) There shall be no appeal under this section on the subject of costs only.

(4) Every appeal under this section shall be preferred within a [period of ninety days] from the date of the decree or order.

----

55. Inserted by Act 49 of 2001, S.9 (w.e.f.24-9-2001).

56. Substituted by Act 68 of 1976, S.19, for S.28 (w.e.f.27-5-1976).

57. Substituted by Act 50 of 2003, S.5, for "period of thirty days" (w.e.f.23-12-2003). S.6 of the Marriage Laws (Amendment) Act, 2003 provides as under:- "6. Transitory provisions.- All decrees and orders made by the Court in any proceedings under the Special Marriage Act or the Hindu Marriage Act shall be governed under the provisions contained in section 3 or section 5, as the case may be, as if this Act came into operation at the time of the institution of the suit.

Provided that nothing in this section shall apply to a decree or order in which the time for appealing has expired under the Special Marriage Act or the Hindu Marriage Act at the commencement of this Act."

Condonation of delay in filing appeal, is permissible: Ratan Malla v. Sefali Malla A.I.R. 2004 Gau. 36 (D.B.).

28-A. Enforcement of decrees and orders:- All decrees and orders made by the Court in any proceeding under this Act shall be enforced in the like manner as the decrees and orders of the Court made in the exercise of its original civil jurisdiction for the time being are enforced.]

CHAPTER VI
SAVINGS AND REPEALS

29. Savings:- (1) A marriage solemnized between Hindus before the commencement of this Act, which is otherwise valid, shall not be deemed to be invalid or even to have been invalid by reason only of the fact that the parties thereto belonged to the same gotra or pravara or belonged to different religions, castes or sub-divisions of the same caste.

(2) Nothing contained in this Act shall be deemed to affect any right recognized by custom or conferred by any special enactment to obtain the dissolution of a Hindu marriage, whether solemnized before or after the commencement of this Act.

(3) Nothing contained in this Act shall affect any proceeding under any law for the time being in force for declaring any marriage to be null and void or for annulling or dissolving any marriage or for judicial separation pending at the commencement of this Act, and any such proceeding may be continued and determined as if this Act had not been passed.

(4) Nothing contained in this Act shall be deemed to affect the provisions contained in the Special Marriage act, 1954 (43 of 1954) with respect to marriage between Hindus solemnized under that Act, whether before or after the commencement of this Act.

Objects and Reasons:- This clause expressly saves, inter alia, customs and special enactments like the Madras Marumakkattayam Act (12 of 1933) which provides for termination of Hindu marriage in any other manner. It is also provides that marriages solemnized under the Special Marriage Act, 1872, are not effected by any thing contained in this Bill. (Now see Special Marriage Act, 1954).

30. Repeals:- {Repealed by the Repealing and Amending Act, 1960 (58 of 1960), section 2 and Schedule (w.e.f. 26-12-1960).}

THE HINDU SUCCESSION ACT, 1956

(30 of 1956)

[17th June, 1956]

CONTENTS

THE HINDU SUCCESSION ACT, 1956[1]

(Act No. 30 of 1956)

[17th June, 1956]

An Act to amend and codify the law relating to intestate succession among Hindus.

Be it enacted by Parliament in the Seventh Year of Republic of India as follows:

CHAPTER I
PRELIMINARY

1. **Short title and extent. -**

(a) This Act may be called the Hindu succession Act, 1956.

(b) It extends to the whole of India except the State of Jammu and Kashmir..

2. **Application of Act-**

(1) This Act applies-

(a) To any persons who is a Hindu by religion in any of its forms or developments including a Virashaiva, a Lingayat or a follower of the Brahmo, Prathana or Arya Samaj;

(b) To any person who is Buddhist, Jaina or Sikh by religion; and

(c) To any other person who is not a Muslim, Christian, Parsi or Jew by religion unless it is proved that any such persons would not have been governed by the Hindu law or by any custom or usage as part of that law in respect of any of the matters dealt with herein if this Act had not been passed.

Explanation. -The following persons are Hindu, Buddhists, Jainas or Sikhs by religion, as the case may be:

(a) Any child, legitimate or illegitimate, both of whose parents are Hindus, Buddhists, Jainas or Sikhs by religion;

(b) Any child, legitimate or illegitimate one of whose parents is a Hindu, Buddhist, Jaina or Sikh by religion and who is brought tip as a member of the tribe community, group of family to which such parent belongs or belonged;

(c) Any person who is a convert or reconvert to the Hindu, Buddhist, Jaina or Sikh religion.

(2) Notwithstanding anything contained in subsection (1), nothing contained in this Act shall apply to the members of any Scheduled Tribe within the

meaning of cleanse (25) of article 366 of the Constitution unless die Central Government, by notification the official Gazette, otherwise directs.

(3)   The expression "Hindu" in any portion of this Act shall be construed as if it included a person who, though not a Hindu by religion is, nevertheless, a person to whom this Act applies by virtue of the provision contained in this section.

STATE AMENDMENTS

Pondicherry. – In Sec. 2 after sub-section (2) the following sub-section shall be inserted:

"(2-A) Notwithstanding anything contained in sub-section (1), nothing contained in this Act, shall apply to the renoncants of the Union Territory of pondicherry.

3.   **Definitions and interpretations.** –

(1)   In this Act, unless the context otherwise requires,-

(a)   "Agnate"-one person is said to be an "agnate" of another if the two are related by blood or adoption wholly through males;

(b)   "Aliyasantana law" means the system of law applicable to persons who, if this Act had not been passed, would have been governed by the Madras Aliyasantana Act, 1949, or by the customary Aliyasantana law with respect to die matter for which provision is made in this Act;

(c)   "Cognate"-one person is said to be a cognate of another if the two are related by blood or adoption but not wholly through males;

(d)   The expression "custom" and "usage" signify any rule which having been continuously and uniformly observed for a long time, has obtained the force of law among Hindus in any local area, tribe, community, group or family:

Provided that the rule is certain and not unreasonable or opposed to public policy; and

Provided further that; in the case of a rule applicable only to a family it has been discontinued by the family;

(e)   "Full blood", "half blood" and "uterine blood"-

(i)   Two, person are said to be related to each other by full blood when they are descended from a common ancestor by the same wife, and by half blood when they, are descended from a common ancestor but; b different wives;

(ii)   Two persons are said to be related to each other by uterine blood when different husbands descend them from a common ancestress but

Explanation. -In this clause "ancestor" includes the father and "ancestress" the other;

(f)   "Heir" means any person, male or female, who is entitled to succeed to the property of an intestate under this Act;

(g)   "Intestate", a person is deemed to die intestate in respect of property of which he or she has not made a testamentary disposition capable of taking effect;

(h)   "Marumakkattayam law" means the system of law applicable to persons-

(a)   Who, if this Act had not been passed would have been governed by the Madras Marumakkattayam Act, 1932; the Travancore Nayar Act; the Travancore Ezhava Act; the Travancore Nanjinad Vellala Act; the Travancore Kshatriya Act; the Travancore Krishnavaka Marumakkathayee Act; the Cochin Marumakkathanyam Act; or the Cochin Nayar Act with respect to the matters for which provision is made in this Act; or

(b)   Who belong to any community, the members of which are largely domiciled in the State of Travancore-Cochin or Madras [as it existed immediately before the lst November, 1956, and who, if this Act had not been passed, would have been governed with respect to the matters for which provision is made in this Act by any system of inheritance in which descent is raced through the female lie;

But does not include the aliyasantana law;

(c)   "Nambudri law" means the system of law applicable to persons who, if this Act had not been passed, would have been governed by the Madras Nambudri Act, 1932; the Cochin Nambudri Act; or the Travancore Malayala Brahmin Act with respect to the matters for which provision is made in this Act;

(d)   "Related" means related by legitimate kinship:

Provided that illegitimate children shall be deemed to be related to their mothers and o one another, and their legitimate descendants shall be deemed to be related to them, and to one another; and any word expressing relationship or denoting a relative shall be construed accordingly.

(2)   In this Act, unless the context otherwise requires, words importing the masculine ender shall not be taken to include females.

1.   Ins. by the Adapation of Laws (No. 3) order, 1956.

4.   **Over-riding effect of Act. –**

(1)   Save as otherwise expressly provided in this Act,-

(a)   Any text, rule or interpretation of Hindu law or any custom or usage as part of that law in force immediately before the commencement of this Act shall cease to have effect with respect to any matter for which provision is made in this Act;

(b)   Any other law in force immediately before the commencement of this Act shall cease to apply to Hindus in so far as it is inconsistent with any of the provisions contained in this Act.

(2)   For the removal of doubts it is hereby declared that nothing contained in this Act shall be deemed to affect the provision of any law for the time being in force providing for the prevention of fragmentation of agricultural holdings or for the fixation of ceilings or for the devolution of tenancy rights in respect of such holdings.

CHAPTER-II
INTESTATE SUCCESSION

GENERAL

5.   **Act not to apply to certain properties. -**

This Act shall not apply to-

(i)   Any property succession to which is regulated by the Indian Succession Act, 1925, by reason of the provisions contained in Section 21 of the Special Marriage Act, 1954;

(ii)   Any estate which descends to a single heir by the terms of any covenant or agreement entered into by the Ruler of any Indian State with the Government of India or by the terms of any enactment passed before the commencement of this Act;

(iii)   The Valiamma Thampuran Kovilagam Estate and the Palace Fund administered by the Palace Administration Board by reason of the powers conferred by Proclamation (IX of 1124) dated 29th June, 1949, promulgated by the Maharaja of Cochin.

6.   **Devolution of interest of coparcenary property. –**

When a male Hindus dies after the commencement of this Act, having at the time of his death an interest in a Mitakshara coparcenary property, his interest in the property shall devolve by survivorship upon the surviving members of the coparcenary and not in accordance with this Act:

Provided that, if the deceased had left him surviving a female relative specified in class I of the Schedule or a male relative specified in that class who claims through such female relative, the interest of the deceased in the Mitakshara coparcenary property shall devolve by testamentary or intestate succession, as the case may be, under this Act and not by survivorship.

Explanation 1. -For the purposes of this section, die interest of a Hindu Mitakshara coparcener shall be deemed to be the share in the property that would have been allotted to him if a partition of the property had taken place immediately before this death, irrespective of whether he was entitled to claim partition or not.

Explanation 2. -Nothing contained in the proviso to this section shall be construed as enabling a person who has separated himself from the coparcenary before the death of the deceased or any of his heirs to claim on intestacy a share in the interest referred to therein.

STATE AMENDMENTS

Karnataka: In its application to the State of Karnataka after Sec. 6 the following section shall be inserted namely, -

"**6-A.   Equal rights to daughter in coparcenary property:**

Notwithstanding anything contained in Sec. 6 of this Act.

(a)   In a joint Hindu family governed by Mitakshara law, the daughter of a coparcener in her own right in the same manner as the son and have the same rights in the coparcenary property as she would have had if she had a son, inclusive of the right to claim by survivorship, and shall be subject to the same liabilities and disabilities in respect thereto as the son.

(b)   At a partition in such a joint Hindu family the coparcenary property shall be so divided as to allot to a daughter the same share, as is allotable to a son.

Provided that the share which a predeceased son or predeceased daughter would have got at the partition if he or she had been alive at the time of the partition, shall be allotted to the surviving child of such predeceased son or such predeceased daughter.

Provided further that the share allotable to the predeceased child of a predeceased son or of a predeceased daughter, if such child had been alive at the time the partition, shall be allotted to the child of such predeceased child of the predeceased son or of such predeceased daughter, as the case may be;

(c)   Any property to which a female Hindu becomes entitled by virtue of the provisions of Cl. (a) shall be held by her with the incidents of coparcenary ownership and shall be regarded, notwithstanding anything contained in this Act or any other law for the time being in force, as property capable of being disposed of by her by will or other testamentary disposition.

(d)   Notwithstanding in Cl. (b) shall apply to a daughter married prior to or to a partition which had been effected before the commencement of Hindu Succession (Karnataka Amendment) Act, 1990.

6-B.   **Interest to devolve by survivorship on death: -**

When a female Hindu dies after the commencement of the Hindu Succession (Karnataka Amendment) Act, 1990), having at the time of her death an interest in a Mitakshara coparcenary property, her interest in the property shall devolve by survivorship upon the surviving members of the coparcenary and not in accordance with this Act:

Provided that if the deceased had left any child or child or a predeceased chil, the interest of the deceased in the Mitakshara coparcenary property shall devolve by testamentary or intestate succession, as the case may be, under this Act and not by survivorship.

Explanation: -(1)   For the purposes of this section, interest of female Hindu Mitakshara Coparcencer shall be deemed to be the share in the property that would have been allotted to her if a partition of the property had taken place immediately before her death irrespective of whether she was entitled to claim partition or not.

(2)   Nothing contained in the proviso to this section shall be construed as enabling a person who, before the death of the deceased had separated himself or herself from the coparcenary, or of his or her heirs to claim on intestacy a share in the interest referred to therein.

6-C.   **Preferential right of acquire property in certain cases. –**

(1)   Where, after the commencement of Hindu Succession (Karnataka Amendment) Act, 1990 an interest in any immovable property of an intestate or in any business carried on by him or her, whether solely or in conjunction with others devolves under Sec. 6-A or 6-B upon two or more heirs, and any one of such heirs proposes to transfer him or her interest in

the property or business, the other heirs shall have a preferential right to acquire the interest proposed to be transferred.

(2)   The consideration for which any interest in the property of the deceases may be transferred under sun-section (1) shall, in the absence of any agreement between the parties, be determined by the Court on application being made to it in this behalf, and if any person proposing to acquire the interest is not willing to acquire it for the consideration so determined, such person shall be liable to pay all costs of or incidental to the application.

(3)   If there are two or more heirs proposing to acquire any interest under this section, that heir who offers the highest consideration for the transfer shall be preferred.

Explanation: - In this section "Court" means the Court within the limits of whose jurisdiction the immovable property is situate or the business is carried on and includes any other Court which the State Government may, by notification in the Official Gazette specify in this behalf.[1]

1.   Vide Knt. Act 23 of 1994.

7.   **Devolution of interest in the property of a tarwad, tavazhi, kutumba, kavaru or illom: -.**

(1)   When a Hindu to whom the marumakkattayam or nambudri law would have; applied if this Act had not been passed dies after the commencement of this Act, having at the time of his or her death all interest in the property of a tarwar, tavazhi or illom, as the case may be, his or her interest in the property shall devolve by testamentary or intestate succession, as the case may be, under this Act and not according to the marumakkattayam or nambudri law.

    Explanation. -For the purposes of this sub-section, the interest of a Hindu in the property of a tarwad, tavazhi or illom shall be deemed to be the share in the property of the tarwad, tavazhi or illom, as the case may be, that would have fallen to him or her if a partition of that property per capita had been made immediately before his or her death among all the members of tarwad, tavazhi or illom, as the case may be, then living, whether he or she was entitled to claim such partition or not under the marumakkattayam or nambudri law applicable to him or her, and such share shall be deemed to have been allotted to him or her absolutely.

(2)   When a Hindu to whom the aliyasantana law would have applied if this Act had not been passed, dies after the commencement of this Act, having at the time of his or her death an undivided interest in the property of a kutumba or kavaru, as the case may be, his or her interest in the property shall devolve by testamentary or intestate succession, as the case may be, under this Act and not according to the aliyasantana law.

Explanation. -For the purpose of this subsection, the interest of a Hindu in the property of kutumba or kavaru shall be deemed to be the share in the property of the kutumba or kavaru as the case may be, that would have fallen to him or her if a partition of that property per capita had been made immediately before his or her death among all the members of the kutumba or kavaru, as the case may be, then living, whether he or she was entitled to claim such partition or not under the aliyasantana law, and such share shall be deemed to have been allotted to him or her absolutely.

(3) Notwithstanding anything contained in sub-section (1), when a sthanamdar dies after the commencement of this Act, sthanam property held by him shall devolve upon the members of the family to which the sthanamdar belonged and the heirs of the sthanamdar as if the sthanam property had been divided per capita immediately before the death of the sthanamdar among himself and all the members of his family then living, and the shares falling to the members of his family and the heirs of the sthanamdar shall be held by them as their separate property.

Explanation. -For the purpose of this subsection, the family of a sthanamdar shall include every, branch of that family, whether divided or undivided, the mate members of which would have been entitled by any custom or usage to succeed to the position of sthanamdar if this Act had not been passed.

STATE AMENDMENTS

Kerala: In sec. 7 of the Hindu Succession Act, 1956, in its application to the State of Kerala.

(a) In sub-section (3) between the words "him" and "shall" the words "or her", between the words "himself" and "and" the words "or herself" and between the words "his" and "family" in two places where they occur the words "or her" shall be respectively inserted.

(b) In the explanation to sub-section (3) the words "male" shall be omitted.

(c) The existing explanation to sub-section (3) shall be numbered as Expl. I and the following shall be added as Expl. II

"Explanation II: The devolution of sthanam properties under sun-section (3) and their division among the members of the family and heirs shall not be deemed to have conferred upon them in respect of immovable properties any higher right sthanamdar regarding eviction or otherwise as against tenants who were holding such properties under the sthani."[1]

1. Vide kerala Act, 1958 (28 of 1958), sec. 27 (w.e.f. 18 May 1959).

8. **General rules of succession in the case of males. -**

The property of a male Hindu dying intestate shall devolve according to the provisions of this Chapter-

(a) Firstly, upon the heirs, being the relatives specified in class I of the Schedule;

(b) Secondly, if there is no heir of class II then upon the heirs, being the relatives specified in class II of the Schedule;

(c) Thirdly, if there is no heir of any of the two classes, then upon the agitates of the deceased; and

(d) Lastly, if there is no agnate, then upon the cognates of the deceased.

9. Orders of succession among heirs in the Schedule.-

Among the heirs specified in the Schedule, those in class I shall take simultaneously and to the exclusion of all other heirs; those in the first entry in class II shall be preferred to those in the second entry; those in the second entry shall be preferred to those in the third entry; and so on in succession.

10. Distributions, of property among heirs in class I of the Schedule. -

The property of an intestate shall be divided among the heirs in class I of the Schedule in accordance with the following rules:

Rule 1. - The intestate's widow, or if there are more widows than one, all the widows together, shall take one share.

Rule 2. - The surviving sons and daughters and the mother of the intestate shall each take one share.

Rule 3. - The heirs in the branch of each pre-deceased son or each pre-deceased daughter of the intestate shall take between them one share.

Rule 4. - The distribution of the share referred to in Rule 3-

(i) Among the heirs in the branch of the pre-deceased son shall be so made that his widow (or widows together) and the Surviving sons and daughters gets equal portions; and the branch of his predeceased sons gets the same portion;

(ii) Among the heirs in the branch of pre-deceased daughter shall be so made that the surviving sons and daughters get equal portions.

11. Distribution of property among heirs in class II of the Schedule. -

The property of an intestate shall be divided between the heirs specified in any one entry in class II of the Schedule so that they share equally.

12. Order of succession among agnates and cognates.-

The order of succession among agnates or cognates, as the case may be, shall be determined in accordance with the rules of preference laid down hereunder:

Rule 1. -   Of two heirs, the one who has fewer or no degrees of ascent is preferred.

Rule 2. -   Where the number of degrees of ascent is the same or none, that heir is preferred who has fewer or no degree of descent.

Rule 3. -   Where neither heirs is entitled to be preferred to the other under Rule 1 or Rule 2 they take simultaneously.

13.   **Computation of degress.** -

(1)   For the purpose of determining the order of succession among agnates or cognates, relationship shall be reckoned from the intestate to the heir in terms of degrees of ascent or degrees of descent or both, as the case may be.

(2)   Degrees of ascent and degrees of descent shall be computed inclusive of the intestate.

(3)   Every generation constitutes a degree either ascending or descending.

14.   **Property of a female Hindu to be her absolute Property.** -

(1)   Any property possessed by a female Hindu, whether acquired before or after the commencement of this Act, shall be held by her as full owner thereof and not as a limited owner.

Explanation. -In this sub-section, "property" includes both movable and immovable property acquired by a female Hindu by inheritance or devise, or at a partition, or in lieu of arrears of maintenance, or by gift from any person, whether a relative or not, before, at or after her marriage, or by her own skill or exertion, or by purchase or by prescription, or in any other manner whatsoever, and also any such property held by her as stridhana immediately before the commencement of this Act.

(2)   Nothing contained in sub-section (1) shall apply to any property acquired by way of gift or under a will or any other instrument or under a decree or order of a civil court or under an award where the terms of the gift, will or other instrument or the decree, order or award prescribe a restricted estate in such property.

15.   **General rules of succession in the case of female Hindus.** -

(1)   The property of a female Hindu dying intestate shall devolve according to the rules set out ill section 16,-

(a)   Firstly, upon the sons and daughters (including the children of any pre-deceased son or daughter) and the husband;

(b)   Secondly, upon the heirs of the husband;

(c)   Thirdly, upon the mother and father;

(d)   Fourthly, upon the heirs of the father; and

(e)   Lastly, upon the heirs of the mother.

(2)   Notwithstanding anything contained in subsection (1),-

(a)   Any property inherited by a female Hindu from tier father or mother shall devolve, in the absence of any son or daughter of the deceased (including the children of any pre-deceased son or daughter) not upon the other heirs referred to in sub-section (1) in the order specified therein, but upon the heirs of the father; and

(b)   Any property inherited by a female Hindu from tier husband or from her father-in-law shall devolve, in the absence of any son or daughter of the deceased (including the children of any pre-deceased son or daughter) not upon the other heirs referred to in subsection (1) in the order specified therein, hill upon the heirs of the husband.

16.   **Order of succession and manner of distribution among heirs of a female Hindu-**

The order of succession among the heirs referred to in Section 15 shall be and the distribution of the intestate's property among those heirs shall take place according, to the following rules, namely:

Rule 1. -   Among the heirs specified in subsection (1) of Section 15, those in one entry shall be preferred to those in any succeeding entry and those including in the same entry shall take simultaneously.

Rule 2. -   If any son or daughter of the intestate had pre-deceased the intestate leaving his or her own children alive at the time of the intestate's death, the children of such son or daughter shall take between them the share which such son or daughter would have taken if living at the intestate's death.

Rule 3. -   The devolution of the property of the intestate on the heirs referred to in clauses (b), (d) and (e) of sub-section (1) and in subsection (2) to Section 15 shall be in the same order and according to the same rules as would have applied if the property had been the father's or the mother's or the husband's as the case may be, and such person had died intestate in respect thereof immediately after the intestate's death.

17.   **Special provisions respecting persons governed by "marumakkattayam and aliyasantana" laws. -**

The provisions of Sections 8, 10, 15 and 23 shall have effect ill relation to persons would have been governed by the marumakkattayam law or aliyasantana law if this Act had not been passed as if-

(i)   For sub-clauses (c) and (d) of Section 8, the following had been substituted. namely :

"(c)   Thirdly, if there is no heirs of any of the two classes, then upon his relatives, whether agitates or cognates";

(ii)   For clauses (a) to (e) of sub-section (1) of Section, 15, the following had been substituted, namely:

"(a)   Firstly, upon the sons and daughters (including the children of any pre-deceased son or daughter) and die mother;

(b)   Secondly, upon the father and the husband.

(c)   Thirdly, upon the heirs of the mother;

(d)   Fourthly, upon the heirs of the father; and

(e)   Lastly, upon the heirs of the husband.";

(iii)   Clause (a) of subsection (2) of Section 15 had been omitted;

(iv)   Section 23 had been omitted.

GENERAL PROVISIONS RELATING TO SUCCESSION

18.   **Full blood preferred to half blood. -**

Heirs related to an intestate by full blood shall be preferred to heirs related by half blood, if the nature of the relationship is the same in every other respect.

19.   **Mode of succession of two or more heirs.**

If two or more heirs succeed together to the property of an intestate, they shall take the property, -

(a)   Save as otherwise expressly provided in this Act, per capita and not per stripes; and

(b)   As tenants-in-common and not as joint tenants.

20.   **Right of child in womb. -**

A child who was in the womb at the time of the death of an intestate and who is subsequently born alive have the same right to inherit to the intestate as if he or she had been born before the death of the intestate, and the inheritance shall be deemed to vest in such a case with effect from the date of the death of the intestate.

21.   **Presumption in cases of simultaneous deaths. -**

Where two persons have died in circumstances rendering it uncertain whether either of them, and if so which, survived the other then, for all purposes affecting succession to property, it shall be presumed, until the contrary is proved, that the younger survived the elder.

22.   **Preferential right to acquire property in certain cases. –**

(1)   Where, after the commencement of this Act, interest in any immovable property of an intestate, or in any business carried on by him or her, whether solely or in conjunction with others, devolve upon two or more heirs specified in class I of the Schedule, and any one of such heirs purposes to transfer his or her interest in the property or business, the other heirs shall have a preferential right to acquire the interest proposed to be transferred.

(2)   The consideration for which any interest in the property of the deceased may be transferred under this section shall, in the absence of any agreement between the parties, be determined by the Court on application being made to it in this behalf, and if any person proposing to acquire the interest is not willing to acquire it for the consideration so determined, such person shall be liable to pay all costs of or incident to the application.

(3)   If there are two or more heirs specified in class I of the Schedule proposing to acquire any interest under this section, that heir who offers the highest consideration for the transfer shall be preferred.

Explanation. -In this section, "court" means the court within the limits of whose jurisdiction the immovable property is situate or the business is carried on, and includes any other court which the State Government may, by notification in the Official Gazette, specify in this behalf.

23.   **Special provision respecting dwelling houses: -**

Where a Hindu intestate has left surviving him or her both male and female heirs specified in class I of the Schedule and his or her property includes a dwelling-house wholly occupied by members of his or her family, then, notwithstanding anything contained in this Act, the right of any such female heir to claim partition of the dwelling-house shall not arise until the male heirs choose to divide their respective shares therein; but the female heir shall be entitled to a right of residence therein :

Provided that where such female heir is a daughter, she shall be entitled to a right of residence in the dwelling-house only if she is unmarried or has been deserted by or has separated from her husband or is a widow.

24. **Certain widows re-marrying may not inherit as widows. -**

Any heir who is related to all intestate as the widow of a pre-deceased soil, the widow of a pre-deceased Son of a pre-deceased son or the widow of a brother shall not be entitled to succeed to the property of the intestate as such widow, if oil the date the succession opens, she has re-married.

25. **Murdered disqualified. -**

A person who commits murder or abets the commission of murder shall be disqualified from inheriting the property of the person murdered, or any other property in furtherance of the succession to which he or she committed or abetted the commission of the murder.

26. **Convert's descendants disqualified. -**

Where, before or after the commencement of this Act, a Hindu has ceased or ceases to be Hindu by conversion to another religion, children both to him or her after such conversion and their descendants shall be disqualified from inheriting the property of any of their Hindu relatives, unless such children or descendants are Hindus at the time when the succession opens.

27. **Succession when heir disqualified. -**

If any person is disqualified from inheriting any property under this Act, it shall devolve as if such person had died before the intestate.

28. **Disease, defect, etc. not to disqualify.-**

No person shall be disqualified from succeeding to any property on the ground of any disease, defect or deformity, or Save as provided in this Act, on any other ground whatsoever.

ESCHEAT

29. **Failure of heirs.-**

If an intestate has left no heir qualified to succeed to his or her property in accordance with the provisions of this Act, such property shall devolve on the government; and the government shall take the property subject to all the obligations and liabilities to which all heir would have been subject.

STATE AMENDMETNS

Andhra pradesh: -   In the Hindu Succession Act, 1956 (herein after referred to as this Act) after Chapter II, the following Chapter shall be inserted, namely: [1]

1.   Ins. by Act No. 13 of 1986, Sec. 2 (w.e.f. 5th September, 1985)

"CHAPTER II-A
SUCCESSION BY SURVIVORSHIP

29-A. Equal rights to daughter in coparcenary property: -

Notwithstanding anything contained in Sec. 6 of this Act, -

(i)   In a join Hindu Family governed by Mitakshara law, the daughter of a coparcener in her own right in the same manner as the son and have the same rights in the coparcenary property as she would have had if she had been a son, inclusive of the right to claim by survivorship; and shall be subject to the same liabilities and disabilities in respect thereto as the son.

(ii)   At a partition in such a joint Hindu family the coparcenary property shall be so divided as to allot to a daughter the same share, as is allotable to a son;

Provided that the share which a pre-deceased son or a pre-deceases daughter would have got at the partition if he or she had been alive at the time of the partition shall be allotted to the surviving child of such pre-deceased son or of such pre-deceased daughter;

Provided further that the share allotable to the predeceased child of a pre-deceased son or of a pre-deceased daughter, if such child had been alive at the time of the partition, shall be allotted to the child of such pre-deceased child of the pre-deceased son or of the pre-deceased daughter as the case may be;

(iii)   Any property to which a female Hindu becomes entitled by virtue of the provisions of Cl. (i) shall be held by her with the incidents of coparcenary ownership and shall be regarded, notwithstanding anything contained in this Act or any other law for the time being in force, as property capable of being disposed of by her by will or other testamentary disposition;

(iv)   Nothing in Cl. (iii) shall apply to prior a daughter married to or to a partition which had been effected before the commencement of the Hindu Succession (Andhra Pradesh Amendment) Act, 1986.

Explanation. -In this section "Court" means the Court within the limits of whose jurisdiction the immoveable property is situate or the business is carried on, and includes any other Court which the State, Government may, by notification in the Andhra Pradesh Gazette, specify in this behalf."

Maharashtra. –Insertion of Chapter II-in Act 30 of 1956. -After Sec. 29 of the Hindu Succession Act, 1956 (30 of 1956), in its application to the State of Maharashtra (hereinafter referred to as "as principal Act", the following Chapter shall be inserted, namely:--

"CHAPTER II-A
Succession by Survivorship

29-A. Equal rights to daughter in coparcenary property. -

Notwithstanding anything contained in Sec.6 of this Act, -

(i)   In a Joint Hindu Family governed by the Mitakshara Law, the daughter of a coparcener shall by birth become a coparcener in her own right in the same manner as a son and have the same rights in the coparcenary property as she would have if she had been a son, inclusive of the right to claim by survivorship; and shall be subject to the same liabilities and disabilities in respect thereto as the son;

(ii)   At a partition in a Joint Hindu Family referred to in Cl. (i), the coparcenary property shall be so divided as to allot to a daughter the same share, as is allotable to a son;

Provided that the share which a pre-deceased son or a pre-deceased daughter would have got at the partition if he or she had been alive at the time of partition shall be allotted to the surviving child of such pre-deceased son or of such pre-deceased daughter:

Provided further that the share allotable to the predeceased child of a pre-deceased son or a pre-deceased daughter, if such child had been alive at the time of the partition, shall be allotted to the child of such predeceased child of the pre-deceased son or of the pre-deceased daughter, as the case may be;

(iii)   Any property to which a female Hindu becomes entitled by virtue of the provisions of Cl. (i) shall be held by her with the incidents of coparcenary, ownership and shall be regarded, notwithstanding anything contained in this Act or any other law for the time being in force, as property capable of being disposed of by her by will or other testamentary disposition;

(iv)   Nothing in this Chapter shall apply to a daughter married before the date of the commencement of the Hindu Succession (Maharashtra Amendment) Act,. 1994 (Mah. XL of 1994) ;

(v)   Nothing in Cl. (ii) shall apply to a partition, which has been effected before the date of commencement of the Hindu Succession (Maharashtra Amendment) Act, 1994.

29-B. Interest to devolve by survivorship on death. -

When a female Hindu dies after the date of the commencement of the Hindu Succession (Maharashtra Amendment) Act, 1994 (Mah XL of 1994), having at the time of her death, an interest in a Mitakshtra coparcenary property by virtue of the provisions of Sec. 29-A, her interest in the property shall devolve by survivorship upon the surviving members of the coparcenary and not in accordance with this Act:

Provided that if the deceased had left any child or child of a pre-deceased child, the interest of the deceased in the Mitakshara coparcenary property shall devolve by testamentary or intestate succession, as the case may be, under this Act and not by survivorship.

Explanation I. -For the purposes of this section, the interest of a female Hindu Mitakshara coparcener shall be deemed to be the share in the property that would have been allotted to her if a partition of the property had taken place immediately before her death, irrespective of whether she was entitled to claim partition or not-

Explanation II. -Nothing contained in the proviso to this section shall be construed as enabling a person who, before the death of the deceased, had separated himself or herself from the coparcenary or any of his heirs to claim on intestacy a share in the interest referred to therein.

29-C. Preferential right to acquire property in certain cases.-

(I) Where, after the date of the commencement of the Hindu Succession (Maharashtra Amendment) Act, 1994 (Mah. .XL 1994), an interest in any immovable property of an intestate or in any business carried on by him or her, whether solely or in conjunction with others, devolves under Sec. 29-A or Sec. 29-B upon two or more heirs, and any one of such heirs proposes to transfer her or his interest in the property or business, the other heirs shall have a preferential right to acquire the interest proposed to be transferred.

(2) The consideration for which any interest in the property of the deceased may be transferred under this section shall, in the absence of any agreement between the parties, be determined by the Court on an application being made to it in this behalf, and if any person proposing to acquire the interest is not willing to acquire it for the consideration so determined, such person shall be liable to pay all costs of, or incident to, the application.

(3) If there are two or more heirs proposing to acquire an interest under this section, then, the heir who offers the highest consideration for the transfer shall be preferred.

Explanation. - In this section "Court" means the Court within the limits of whose jurisdiction the immovable property is situate or the business is carried on, and includes any other Court, which the State Government may, by notification in the Official Gazette, specify in this behalf.[1]

Tamil Nadu. - In the Hindu Succession Act, 1956 (hereinafter referred to as this Act) after Chapter II, the following "Chapter II-A" shall be 'inserted, namely, -

1. Vide Maharashtra Act. No. XL of 1994, sec. 2 punished in the Maharashtra Government Gazette, Extraordinary, pt. IV dated December, 1994.

CHAPTER-IIA

SUCCESSION BY SURVIVORSHIP
[SAME AS OF ANDHRA PRADESH][1]

1. Vide Tamil Nadu Act, 1990 (Act 1 of 1990) w.e.f.25th March, 1989]

CHAPTER III
TESTAMENTARY SUCCESSION

30. Testamentary succession. -

[1][* * *] Any Hindu may dispose of by will or other testamentary disposition any property, which is capable of being so disposed of by him, in accordance with the provisions of the Indian Succession Act, 1925, or any other law for the time being in force and applicable to Hindus.

Explanation. -The interest of a male Hindu in a Mitakshara coparcenary property or the interest of a member of a tarwad, tavazhi, illom, kutumba or kavaru in the property of the tarwad, tavazhi, illom, kutumba or kavaru shall notwithstanding anything contained in this Act or in any other law for the time being in force, be deemed to be property capable of being disposed of by him or by her within the meaning of this [2][section.]

[3][*

1. The brackets and figure "(1)" emitted by Act No. 58 of 1960.
2. Subs. by Act No. 56 of 1974, "sub-section".
3. Sub-section (2) omitted by Act No. 78 of 1956.

CHAPTER IV
REPEALS

31. Repeals. -

[Repealed by Repealing and Amending Act, 1960 (58, of 1960)].

THE SCHEDULE

(See Section 8)
HEIRS IN CLASS I AND CLASS II

CLASS-I

Son; daughter; widow; mother; son of a pre-deceased son; daughter of a pre-deceased son; son of a pre-deceased daughter; daughter of a pre-deceased daughter; widow of it pre-deceased son; son of a pre-deceased son of a pre-deceased soil; daughter of a pre-deceased son of a pre-deceased son; widow of a pre-deceased son of a pre-deceased son.

CLASS- II

I   Father.

II   (1) Son's daughter's son, (2) son's daughter's daughter, (3) brother, (4) sister.

III   (1) Daughter's son's son, (2) daughter's son's daughter, (3) daughter's daughter's son, (4) daughter's daughter's daughter.

IV   (1) Brother's son, (2) sister's son, (3) brother's daughter, (4) sister's daughter.

V   Father's father; father's mother.

VI   Father's widow; brother's widow.

VII   Father's brother; father's sister.

VIII Mother's father; mother's mother.

IX   Mother's brother; mother's sister.

Explanation. -   In this Schedule, references to a brother or sister do not include references to a brother or sister by uterine blood.

Hindu Minority and Guardianship Act, 1956

An Act to amend and codify certain parts of the law relating to minority and guardianship among Hindus.

BE it enacted by Parliament in the Seventh Year of the Republic of India as follows:-

1 . Short title and extent.- (1) This Act may be called the Hindu Minority and Guardianship Act, 1956.

(2) It extends to the whole of India except the State of Jammu Kashmir and applies to Hindus domiciled in the territories to which this Act extends who are outside the said territories.

2 . Act to be supplemental to Act 8 of 1890.- The provisions of this Act shall be in addition to, and not, save as hereinafter expressly provided, in derogation of, the Guardians and Wards Act, 1890 (8 of 1890).

3 . Application of Act.- (1) This Act applies-

(c) to any person who is a Hindu by religion in any of its forms or developments, including a Virashaiva, a Lingayat or a follower of the Brahmo, Prarthana or Arya Samaj.

(d) to any person who is a Buddhist, Jaina or Sikh by religion and

(e) to any person domiciled in the territories to which this Act extends who is not a Muslim, Christian, Parsi, or Jew by religion, unless it is proved that any such person would not have been governed by the Hindu law or by any custom or usage as part of that law in respect of any of the matters dealt with herein if this Act had not been passed.

Explanation.- The following persons are Hindus, Buddhists, Jainas or Sikhs by religion, as the case may be:-

(d)   any child, legitimate or illegitimate, both of whose parents are Hindus, Buddhists, Jainas or Sikhs by religion;

(e) any child, legitimate or illegitimate, one of whose parents is a Hindu, Buddhists, Jaina or Sikh by religion and who is brought up as a member of the tribe, community, group or family to which such parent belongs or belonged; and

(f) any person who is convert or re-convert to the Hindu, Buddhist, Jaina or Sikh religion.

(2) Notwithstanding anything contained in sub-section (1), nothing contained in this Act shall apply to the members of any scheduled Tribe within the meaning of clause (25) of article 366 of the Constitution unless the Central Government, by notification in the Official Gazette, otherwise directs.

(3) The expression 'Hindu' in any portion of this Act shall be construed as if it included a person who, though not a Hindu by religion, is nevertheless, a person to whom this Act, applies by virtue of the provisions contained in this section.

4 . Definitions.- In this Act,-

(c) "minor" means a person who has not completed the age of eighteen years;

> **(d)** "major" means a person having the care of the person of a minor or of his property or of both his person and property, and includes-

(d)   a natural guardian,

(e) a guardian appointed by the will of the minor's father or mother,

(f) a guardian appointed or declared by a court, and

(g) a person empowered to act as such by or under any enactment relating to any court of wards;

(c) "natural guardian" means any of the guardians mentioned in section 6.

5 . Over-riding effect of Act.- Save as otherwise expressly provided in this Act,-

(h)any text, rule or interpretation of Hindu law or any custom or usage as part of that law in force immediately before the commencement of this Act shall cease to have effect with respect to any matter for which provision is made in this Act;

(i) any other law in force immediately before the commencement of this Act shall cease to have effect in so far as it is inconsistent with any of the provisions contained in this Act.

6 . Natural guardians of a Hindu minor.- The natural guardians of a Hindu, minor, in respect of the minor's person as well as in respect of the minor's property (excluding his or her undivided interest in joint family property), are-

(d)in the case of a boy or an unmarried girl-the father, and after him, the mother: provided that the custody of a minor who has not completed the age of five years shall ordinarily be with the mother;

(e) in the case of an illegitimate boy or an illegitimate unmarried girl-the mother, and after her, the father;

(f) in the case of a married girl-the husband;

Provided that no person shall be entitled to act as the natural guardian of a minor under the provisions of this section-

(a) if he has ceased to be a Hindu, or

(b) if he has completely and finally renounced the world by becoming a hermit (vanaprastha) or an ascetic (yati or sanyasi)

Explanation.- In this section, the expressions 'father' and 'mother' do not include a step-father and a step-mother.

7 . Natural guardianship of adopted son.- The natural guardianship of an adopted son who is a minor passes, on adoption, to the adoptive father and after him to the adoptive mother.

8 . Powers of natural guardian.- (1) The natural guardian of a Hindu minor has power, subject to the provisions of this section, to do all acts which are necessary or reasonable and proper for the benefit of the minor or for the realization, protection or benefit of the minor's estate; but the guardian can in no case bind the minor by a personal covenant.

(2) The natural guardian shall not, without the previous permission of the court,-

(d) mortgage or charge, or transfer by sale, gift, exchange or otherwise any part of the immovable property of the minor or

(e) lease any part of such property for a term exceeding five years or for a term extending more than one year beyond the date on which the minor will attain majority.

(d) Any disposal of immovable property by a natural guardian, in contravention of sub-section (1) or sub-section (2), is voidable at the instance of the minor or any person claiming under him.

(e) No court shall grant permission to the natural guardian to do any of the acts mentioned in sub-section (2) except in case of necessity or for an evident advantage to the minor.

(f) The Guardians and Wards Act, 1890 (8 of 1890), shall apply to and in respect of an application for obtaining the permission of the court under sub-section (2) in all respects as if it were an application for obtaining the permission of the court under section 29 of that Act, and in particular-

(e) proceedings in connection with the application shall be deemed to be proceedings under that Act within the meaning of section 4A thereof.

(f) the court shall observe the procedure and have the powers specified in sub-sections (2), (3) and (4) of section 31 of that Act; and

   (g) an appeal lie from an order of the court refusing permission to the natural guardian to do any of the acts mentioned in sub-section (2) of this section to the court to which appeals ordinarily lie from the decisions of that court.

(6) In this section, "Court" means the city civil court or a district court or a court empowered under section 4A of the Guardians and Wards Act, 1890 (8 of 1890), within the

local limits of whose jurisdiction the immovable property in respect of which the application is made is situate, and where the immovable property is situate within the jurisdiction of more than one such court, means the court within the local limits of whose jurisdiction any portion of the property is situate.

9 . Testamentary guardians and their powers.- (1) A Hindu father entitled to act as the natural guardian of his minor legitimate children may, by will appoint a guardian for any of them in respect of the minor's person or in respect of the minor's property (other than the undivided interest referred to in section 12) or in respect of both.

(c) An appointment made under sub-section (1) shall have not effect if the father predeceases the mother, but shall revive if the mother dies without appointing, by will, any person as guardian.

(d) A Hindu widow entitled to act as the natural guardian of her minor legitimate children, and a Hindu mother entitled to act as the natural guardian of her minor legitimate children by reason of the fact that the father has become disentitled to act as such, may, by will, appoint a guardian for any of them in respect of the minor's person or in respect of the minor's property (other than the undivided interest referred to in section 12) or in respect of both.

(e) A Hindu mother entitled to act as the natural guardian of her minor illegitimate children may; by will appoint a guardian for any of them in respect of the minor's person or in respect of the minor's property or in respect of both.

(f) The guardian so appointed by will has the right to act as the minor's guardian after the death of the minor's father or mother, as the case may be, and to exercise all the rights of a natural guardian under this Act to such extent and subject to such restrictions, if any, as are specified in this Act and in the will.

(g) The right of the guardian so appointed by will shall, where the minor is a girl, cease on her marriage.

10 . Incapacity of minor to act as guardian of property.- A minor shall be incompetent to act as guardian of the property of any minor.

11 . De facto guardian not to deal with minors property.- After the commencement of this Act, no person shall be entitled to dispose of, or deal with, the property of a Hindu minor merely on the ground of his or her being the de facto guardian of the minor.

12 . Guardian not to be appointed for minors undivided interest in joint family property.- Where a minor has an undivided interest in joint family property and the property is under the management of an adult member of the family, no guardian shall be appointed for the minor in respect of such undivided interest:

Provided that nothing in this section shall be deemed to affect the jurisdiction of a High Court the welfare of the minor shall be the paramount consideration.

13 . Welfare of minor to be paramount consideration.- (1) In the appointment of declaration of any person as guardian of a Hindu minor by a court, the welfare of the minor shall be the paramount consideration.

(2) No person shall be entitled to the guardianship by virtue of the provisions of this Act or of any law relating to guardianship in marriage among Hindus, if the court is of opinion that his or her guardianship will not be for the welfare of the minor.

THE HINDU ADOPTIONS AND MAINTENANCE ACT, 1956

[Act No.78 of 1956][21st December, 1956]

Be it enacted by Parliament in the Seventh Year of the Republic of India as follows:-

CHAPTER I

PRELIMINARY

1. Short title and extent- (1) This Act may be called the Hindu Adoptions and Maintenance Act, 1956.

(2) It extends to the whole of India except the State of Jammu and Kashmir.

2. Application of Act- (1) This Act applies-

(f)   to any person, who is a Hindu by religion in any of its forms or developments, including a Virashaiva, a Lingayat or a follower of the Brahmo, Prarthana or Arya Samaj,

(g) to any person who is a Buddhist, Jaina or Sikh by religion, and

(h) to any other person who is not a Muslim, Christian, Parsi or Jew by religion unless it is proved that any such person would not have been governed by the Hindu law or by any custom or usage as part of that law in respect of any of the matters dealt with herein if this Act had not been passed.

Explanation - The following persons are Hindus, Buddhists, Jainas or Sikhs by religion, as the case may be:-

(g) any child, legitimate or illegitimate, both of whose parents are Hindus, Buddhists, Jainas or Sikhs by religion;

(h) any child, legitimate for illegitin~ate, one of whose parents is a Hindu, Buddhist, Jaina or Sikh by religion and who is brought up as a member of the tribe, community, group or family to which such parent belongs or belonged,

(bb) any child, legitimate or illegitimate, who has been abandoned both by his father and mother or whose parentage is not known and who is either case is brought up as a Hindu, Buddhist, Jaina or Sikh, and

(c) any person who is a convert or reconvert to the Hindu, Buddhist, Jaina or Sikh, religion.

(2) Notwithstanding anything contained in sub-section (1), nothing contained in this Act shall apply to the members of any Scheduled Tribe within the meaning of clause (25) of Article 366 of the Constitution unless the Central Government,

by notification in the Official Gazette, otherwise directs.

(2 -A) Notwithstanding anything contained in sub-section (1), nothing contained in this Act shall apply to the Renoncants of the Union Territory of Pondicherry.

(3) The expression "Hindu" in any portion of this Act shall be construed as if it included a person who, though not a Hindu by religion, is nevertheless, a person to whom this Act applies by virtue of the provisions contained in this section.

3. Definitions- In this Act unless the context otherwise requires-

(a) the expressions "custom" and "usage" signify any rule which, having been continuously and uniformly observed for a long time, has obtained the force of law among Hindus in any local area, tribe, community, group or family;

Provided that the rule is certain and not unreasonable or opposed to public policy; and

Provided further that, in the case of a rule applicable only to a family, it has not been discontinued by the family;

(b) "maintenance" includes-

(i) in all cases, provision for food, clothing, residence, education and medical attendance and treatment;

(ii) in the case of an unmarried daughter also the reasonable expenses of and incident to her marriage;

(c) "minor" means a person who has not completed his or her age of eighteen years.

4. Overriding effect of Act- Save as otherwise expressly provided in this Act,-

(e) any text, rule or interpretation of Hindu law or any custom or usage as part of that law in force immediately before the commencement of this Act shall cease to have effect with respect to any matter for which provision is made in this Act;

(f) any other law in force immediately before the commencement of this Act shall cease to apply to Hindus in so far as it is inconsistent with any of the provisions contained in this Act.

CHAPTER II

ADOPTION

5. Adoptions to be regulated by this Chapter- (1) No adoption shall be made after the commencement of this Act by or to a Hindu except in accordance with the provisions contained in this Chapter, and any adoption made in contravention of the said provisions shall be void.

(2) An adoption which is void shall neither create any rights in the adoptive

family in favour of any person which he or she could not have acquired except by reason of the adoption, nor destroy the rights of any person in the family of his or her birth.

6. Requisites of a valid adoption- No adoption shall be valid unless-

(h) the person adopting has the capacity, and also the right, to take in adoption;

(i)   the person giving in adoption has the capacity to do so;

(j)   the person adopted is capable of being taken in adoption; and

(k)   the adoption is made in compliance with the other conditions mentioned in this Chapter.

7. Capacity of a male Hindu to take in adoption- Any male Hindu who is of sound mind and is not a minor has the capacity to take a son or a daughter in adoption.

Provided that, if he has a wife living, he shall not adopt except with the consent of his wife unless the wife has completely and finally renounced the world or has ceased to be a Hindu or has been declared by a court of competent jurisdiction to be of unsound mind.

Explanation-If a person has more than one wife living at the time of adoption, the consent of all the wives is necessary unless the consent of any one of them is unnecessary for any of the reasons specified in the preceding proviso.

8. Capacity of a female Hindu to take in adoption- Any female Hindu-

(j)   who is of sound mind,

(k)   who is not a minor, and

(l)   who is not married, or if married, whose marriage has been dissolved or whose husband is dead or has completely and finally renounced the world or has ceased to be a Hindu or has been declared by a court of competent jurisdiction to be of unsound mind,

has the capacity to take a son or daughter in adoption.

9. Persons capable of giving in adoption- (1) No person except the father or mother or the guardian of a child shall have the capacity to give the child in adoption.

(g) Subject to the provisions of sub-section (3) and sub-section (4), the father, if alive, shall alone have the right to give in adoption, but such right shall not be exercised save with the consent of the mother unless the mother has completely and finally renounced the world or has ceased to be a Hindu or has been declared by a court of competent jurisdiction to be of unsound mind.

(h) The mother may give the child in adoption if the father is dead or has completely and finally renounced the world or has ceased to be a Hindu or has been declared by a court of competent jurisdiction to be of unsound mind.

(f)   Where both the father and mother are dead or have completely and finally renounced the world or have abandoned the child or have been declared by a court of competent jurisdiction to be of unsound mind or where the parentage of the child is not known, the guardian of the child may give the child in adoption with the previous permission of the court to any person including the guardian himself.

(g)   Before granting permission to a guardian under sub-section (4) the court shall be satisfied that the adoption will be for the welfare of the child, due consideration being for this purpose given to the wishes of the child having regard to the age and understanding of the child and that the applicant for permission has not received or agreed to receive and that no person has made or given or agreed to make or give to the applicant any payment or reward in consideration of the adoption except such as the court may sanction.

Explanation- For the purposes of this section-

(i) the expressions "father" and "mother" do not include an adoptive father and an adoptive mother,

(i-a) "guardian" means a person having the care of the person of a child or of both his person and property and includes-

(g) a guardian appointed by will of the child's father or mother; and

(h) a guardian appointed or declared by a court; and

(ii) "court" means the city or civil court or a district court within the local limits or whose jurisdiction the child to be adopted ordinarily resides.

10. Persons who may be adopted- No person shall be capable of being taken in adoption unless the following conditions are fulfilled, namely-

(h) he or she is a Hindu;

(i)   he or she has not already been adopted;

(j)   he or she has not been married, unless there is a custom or usage applicable to the parties which permits persons who are married being taken in adoption;

(k)   he or she has not completed the age of fifteen years, unless there is a custom or usage applicable to the parties which permits persons who have completed the age of fifteen years being taken in adoption.

11. Other conditions for a valid adoption- In every adoption, the following conditions must be complied with:

(i) if any adoption is of a son, the adoptive father or mother by whom the adoption is made must not have a Hindu son, son's son or son's son's son (whether by legitimate blood relationship or by adoption) living at the time of adoption;

(h) if the adoption is of a daughter the adoptive father or mother by whom the adoption is made must not have a Hindu daughter or son's daughter (whether by legitimate blood relationship or by adoption) living at the time of adoption;

(i) if the adoption is by a male and the person to be adopted is a female, the adoptive father is at least twenty-one years older than the person to be adopted;

(j) if the adoption is by a female and the person to be adopted is a male, the adoptive mother is at least twenty-one years older than the person to be adopted;

(k) the same child may not be adopted simultaneously by two or more persons;

(l) the child to be adopted must be actually given and taken in adoption by the parents or guardian concerned or under their authority with intent to transfer the child from the family of its birth or in the case of an abandoned child or a child whose parentage is not known, from the place or family where it has been brought up to the family of its adoption.

Provided that the performance of *datta homan,* shall not be essential to the validity of an adoption.

12. Effect of adoptions- An adopted child shall be deemed to be the child of his or her adoptive father or mother for all purposes with effect from the date of the adoption and from such date all the ties of the child in the family of his or her birth shall be deemed to be severed and replaced by those created by the adoption in the adoptive family.

Provided that-

14. the child cannot marry any person whom he or she could not have married if he or she had continued in the family of his or her birth;

15. any property which vested in the adopted child before the adoption shall continue to vest in such person subject to the obligations, if any, attaching to the ownership of such property, including the obligation to maintain relatives in the family of his or her birth;

16. the adopted child shall not divest any person of any estate which vested in him or her before the adoption.

(f) **Right of adoptive parents to dispose of their properties**- Subject to any agreement to the contrary, an adoption does not deprive the adoptive father or mother of the power to dispose of his or her property by transfer *inter vivos* or by will.

(g) **Determination of adoptive mother in certain cases**- (1) Where a Hindu who has a wife living adopts a child she shall be deemed to be the adoptive mother.

(2) Where an adoption has been made with the consent of more than one wife,

the senior most in marriage among them shall be deemed to be the adoptive mother and the others to be stepmothers.

(3) Where a widower or a bachelor adopts a child, any wife whom he subsequently marries shall be deemed to be the stepmother of the adopted child.

(4) Where a widow or an unmarried woman adopts a child, any husband whom she marries subsequently shall be deemed to be the stepfather of the adopted child.

15. **Valid adoption not to be cancelled**- No adoption which had been validly made can be cancelled by the adoptive father or mother or any other person, nor can the adopted child renounce his or her status as such and return to the family of his or her birth.

16. **Presumption as to registered documents relating to adoption**-Whenever any document registered under any law for the time being in force is produced before any court purporting to record an adoption made and is signed by the person giving and the person taking the child in adoption, the court shall presume that the adoption has been made in compliance with the provisions of this Act unless and until it is disproved.

17. **Prohibition of certain payments**- (1) No person shall receive or agree to receive any payment or other reward in consideration of the adoption of any person, and no person shall make or give or agree to make or give to any other person any payment or reward the receipt of which is prohibited by this section.

(2) If any person contravenes the provisions of sub-section (1), he shall be punishable with imprisonment which may extend to six months, or with fine, or with both.

(3) No prosecution under this section shall be instituted without the previous sanction of the State Government or an officer authorized by the State Government in this behalf.

CHAPTER III

MAINTENANCE

18. Maintenance of wife- (1) Subject to the provisions of this section, a Hindu wife, whether married before or after the commencement of this Act, shall be entitled to be maintained by her husband during her lifetime.

(2) A Hindu wife shall be entitled to live separately from her husband without forfeiting her claim to maintenance,-

(a) if he is guilty of desertion, that is to say, of abandoning her without reasonable cause and without her consent or against her wish, or of wilfully neglecting her;

(b) if he has treated her with such cruelty as to cause a reasonable apprehension in her mind that it will be harmful or injurious to live with her husband;

(c) if he is suffering from a virulent form of leprosy;

(d) if he has any other wife living;

(e) if he keeps a concubine in the same house in which his wife is living or habitually resides with a concubine elsewhere;

(f) if he has ceased to be a Hindu by conversion to another religion;

(g) if there is any other cause justifying her living separately.

(3) A Hindu wife shall not be entitled to separate residence and maintenance from her husband if she is unchaste or ceases to be a Hindu by conversion to another religion.

19. Maintenance of widowed daughter-in-law- (1) A Hindu wife, whether married before or after the commencement of this Act, shall be entitled to be maintained after the death of her husband by her father-in-law.

Provided and to the extent that she is unable to maintain herself out of her own earnings or other property or, where she has no property of her own, is unable to obtain maintenance-

(a) from the estate of her husband or her father or mother, or

(b) from her son or daughter, if any, or his or her estate.

(2) Any obligation under sub-section (1) shall not be enforceable if the fatherin-law has not the means to do so from any coparcenary property in his possession out of which the daughter- in-law has not obtained any share, and any such obligation shall cease on the remarriage of the daughter-in-law.

20. Maintenance of children and aged parents- (1) Subject to the provisions of this section a Hindu is bound, during his or her lifetime, to maintain his or her legitimate or illegitimate children and his or her aged or infirm parents.

(2) A legitimate or illegitimate child may claim maintenance from his or her father or mother so long as the child is a minor.

(3) The obligation of a person to maintain his or her aged or infirm parent or daughter who is unmarried extends in so far as the parent or the unmarried daughter, as the case may be, is unable to maintain himself or herself out of his or her own ealnings or other property

Explanation- In this section "parent" includes a childless stepmother.

21. Dependents defined- For the purposes of this Chapter "dependents" mean the following relatives of the deceased-

(i) his or her father;

(ii) his or her mother;

(iii) his widow, so long as she does not remarry;

(iv) his or her son or the son of his predeceased son or the son of a predeceased son of his predeceased son, so long as he is a minor; provided and to the extent that he is unable to obtain maintenance, in the case of a grandson from his father's or mother's estate, and in the case of a great-grandson, from the estate of his father or mother or father's father or father's mother;

(v) his or her unmarried daughter for the unmarried daughter of his predeceased son or the unmarried daughter of a predeceased son of his predeceased son, so long as she remains unmarried; provided and to the extent that she is unable to obtain maintenance, in the case of a grand daughter from her father's or mother's estate and in the case of a great-grand daughter from the estate of her father or mother or father's father or father's mother;

(vi) his widowed daughter; provided and to the extent that she is unable to obtain maintenance-

(a) from the estate of her husband; or

(b) from her son or daughter, if any, or his or her estate; or

(c) from her father-in-law or his father or the estate of either of them;

(vii) any widow of his son or of a son of his predeceased son, so long as she does not remarry; provided and to the extent that she is unable to obtain maintenance from her husband's estate, or from her son or daughter, if any, or his or her estate; or in the case of a grandson's widow, also from her father-in-law's estate;

(viii) his or her minor illegitimate son, so long as he remains a minor;

(xi) his or her illegitimate daughter, so long as she remains unmarried.

22. Maintenance of dependents- (1) Subject to the provisions of sub-section (2), the heirs of a deceased Hindu are bound to maintain the dependents of the deceased out of the estate inherited by them from the deceased.

(2) Where a dependent has not obtained, by testamentary or intestate succession, any share in the estate of a Hindu dying after the commencement of this Act, the dependent shall be entitled, subject to the provisions of this Act, to maintenance from those who take the estate.

(3) The liability of each of the persons who take the estate shall be in proportion to the value of the share or part of the estate taken by him or her.

(4) Notwithstanding anything contained in sub-section (2) or sub-section (3), no person who is himself or herself a dependent shall be liable to contribute to the maintenance of others, if he or she has obtained a share or part, the value of which is, or would, if the liability to contribute were enforced, become less than

what would be awarded to him or her by way of maintenance under this Act.

23. Amount of maintenance- (1) It shall be in the discretion of the court to determine whether any, and if so what, maintenance shall be awarded under the provisions of this Act, and in doing so, the court shall have due regard to the consideration set out in sub-section (2) or sub-section (3), as the case maybe, so far as they are applicable.

(2) In determining the amount of maintenance, if any, to be awarded to a wife, children or aged or infirm parents under this Act, regard shall be had to-

(a) the position and status of the parties;

(b) the reasonable wants of the claimant;

(c) if the claimant is living separately, whether the claimant is justified in doing so;

(d) the value of the claimant's property and any income derived from such property, or from the claimant's own earning or from any other source;

(e) the number of persons entitled to maintenance under this Act.

(3) In determining the amount of maintenance, if any, to be awarded to a dependent under this Act, regard shall be had to-

(a) the net value of the estate of the deceased after providing for the payment of his debts;

(b) the provision, if any, made under a will of the deceased in respect, of the dependent;

(c) the degree of relationship between the two;

(d) the reasonable wants of the dependent;

(e) the past relations between the dependent and the deceased;

(f) the value of the property of the dependent and any income derived from such property, or from his or her earnings or from any other course;

(g) the number of dependents entitled to maintenance under this Act.

24. **Claimant to maintenance should be a Hindu-** No person shall be entitled to claim maintenance under this Chapter if he or she has ceased to be a Hindu by conversion to another religion.

25. **Amount of maintenance may be altered on change of circumstances-**The amount of maintenance, whether fixed by a decree of court or by agreement either before or after the commencement of this Act, may be altered subsequently if there is a material change in the circumstances justifying such alteration.

26. **Debts to have priority**-Subject to the provisions contained in Section 27 debts of every description contracted or payable by the deceased shall have priority over the claims of his dependents for maintenance under this Act.

27. **Maintenance when to be a charge**- A dependent's claim for maintenance under this Act shall not be a charge on the estate of the deceased or any portion thereof, unless one has been created by the will of the deceased, by a decree of court, by agreement between the dependent and the owner of the estate or portion, or otherwise.

28. **Effect of transfer of property on right or maintenance**- where a dependent has a right to receive maintenance out of an estate and such estate or any part thereof is transferred, the right to receive maintenance may be enforced agamst the transferee if the transferee has notice of the right or if the transfer is gratuitous; but not against the transferee for consideration and without notice of the right.

CHAPTER IV

REPEALS AND SAVINGS

29. *Repeals*- [Repealed by Act 58 of 1960].

30. **Savings**- Nothing contained in this Act shall affect any adoption made before the commencement of this Act, and the validity and effect of any such adoption shall be determined as if this Act had not been passed.

www.ingramcontent.com/pod-product-compliance
Lightning Source LLC
Chambersburg PA
CBHW080605180526
45168CB00007B/2784